Contents

Introduction — Setting the scene: some travel facts   vii

1   Travel-related disease — infection and infestation   1

2   Travel-related disease — environmental and climatic   21
     hazards

3   Problems of specific groups of travellers   35

4   Travel vaccinations   61

5   Malaria   77

6   Assessing the risks of travel   95

7   Problems of the returned traveller   105

8   Setting up a travel service in the practice   113

9   Policy and travel health protocols in practice   123
     Karen Howell

Appendix — Information sources   145

References   165

Index   167

Travel Health
for the
Primary Care Team

Dr Mike Townend and Karen Howell

Quay
Books

Mark Allen
Publishing Ltd

Quay Books Division, Mark Allen Publishing Group
Jesses Farm, Snow Hill, Dinton, Wiltshire, SP3 5HN

British Library Cataloguing-in-Publication Data
A catalogue record is available for this book

© Mark Allen Publishing Ltd 1999
ISBN 1 85642 171 6

Printed in the UK by Redwood Books, Trowbridge, Wiltshire

Introduction

Setting the scene: some travel facts

United Kingdom residents made over 41 million visits abroad during 1995. About 37 million of these visits were made to European Community countries, other European countries and North America. However, approximately 4.5 million visits were made to different parts of the world, including tropical and developing countries in Africa, South America, the Indian subcontinent and the Far East. About 26 million trips were for holiday purposes (Office of National Statistics, 1995). As air travel becomes more accessible to more people, holiday travel to such destinations as Thailand, Kenya and Goa is now commonplace, and more exotic locations including African countries, South America, the Caribbean, and Far Eastern countries such as Vietnam, are rapidly becoming popular. In 1996 about eighty per cent of British citizens had either travelled or lived abroad at some time in their lives. In the five years prior to 1996, over half of all British citizens had been abroad and about sixteen per cent of these travellers had been to an area with health risks requiring travel vaccination. During that time, travel to high risk areas increased in each successive year (MORI, 1996).

As the number of travellers setting off abroad progressively increases, there is a corresponding increase in the numbers of those approaching members of the primary care team for advice. Against this background, the speciality of travel medicine is emerging. It deals with increasingly complex itineraries and associated health risks. Travel medicine is concerned with the whole spectrum of health risks for the traveller, which depends on far more factors than merely the country of destination. Travellers must be aware of — and protected against — the diseases commonly found in the country to which they will travel, in the region of the country to which they are going and at the relevant time of year. Travellers also need to be aware of potential hazards in their chosen method of travel, for example air or sea travel. They need to consider the accommodation they will use in relation both to unsatisfactory food and water hygiene, and risks of person-to-person infection. The activities indulged in during the visit may expose the traveller to increased risks. The traveller's age or medical history may increase the risks of travel, or interfere with preventive measures such as vaccination and anti-malarial prophylaxis. The travel health adviser will therefore need to take into account a wide variety of personal, epidemiological and geographical factors in order to give relevant advice, and will also need access to a regularly updated database.

While the primary care team is among the most frequently used for advice by travellers, the information provided is not always perceived as useful or appropriate (Townend, 1998). There is clearly a need for education and information for healthcare professionals who advise travellers, particularly in primary care and also in other fields such as occupational medicine. These professionals require education and information in assessing risks for travellers, and in giving advice and protection. The advice given by travel agents and holiday companies to their clients is often incomplete or inaccurate, and there is a need for members of the industry to be better informed and to give better information to their clients. Travellers need to be educated to present themselves in sufficient time before travelling in order for suitable protective measures to be taken. As many as 44 per cent of travellers to high or medium risk areas do not seek any advice prior to travel (RSL, 1995).

Effects of travel on the host country

When preparing for a journey, the emphasis is usually on the effects that the host country will have upon the traveller. The effects of travellers upon the host country are often overlooked. There are undoubtedly financial benefits to a host country from tourism, but there are also drawbacks. Observation of affluent tourists may lead to the development of unrealistic expectations and consumer demands and this, in turn, may lead to criminal activities in an attempt to fulfil these new expectations. Traditional culture may become corrupted; traditional occupations may lose manpower to tourism; and the unwise distribution of tips and gifts may turn independent people into beggars. There could be some health gains to indigenous people from greater affluence resulting from tourism. However, in some countries sex tourism and travel aimed at much easier access to recreational drugs, particularly by injection, have greatly increased the spread of HIV and other sexually-transmitted diseases. The ease and speed of modern travel may facilitate the spread of disease back to the traveller's country of origin, but it also facilitates the spread of other diseases to the host country. While the main emphasis of this book is on the health and welfare of the traveller, the effects of travel upon the host country and its population should not be overlooked.

1

Travel-related disease — infection and infestation

Sources of infection for the traveller

Food and water

Food

Food may be contaminated with pathogenic organisms at any stage from production to consumption. For example:

- crops may be watered with contaminated water or fertilised with human excrement
- produce may be washed with contaminated water after harvesting
- fish, especially shellfish, may be contaminated by the water that forms its habitat
- meat and poultry may be infected at source or during handling of carcasses
- infected food may be inadequately cooked, resulting in persistence of organisms
- food may be contaminated during serving due to inadequate personal hygiene in food handlers
- the growth of organisms in food may be encouraged by leaving it to stand after cooking, thus making it open to access by flies, or by reheating to a temperature insufficiently high to kill organisms that have gained access to it.

Water

Water supplies in the UK, much of Europe, North America, Australia and New Zealand are usually free of most organisms that are pathogenic for humans. This cannot be guaranteed elsewhere — water purification and also sewage disposal may be less rigorous, haphazard, or even non-existent. It is then relatively easy for faecal micro-organisms to enter drinking water and so lead to the faecal/ oral spread of disease.

Among the diseases that may occur from the ingestion of contaminated water are poliomyelitis, hepatitis A (and E), typhoid and other Salmonella infections such as paratyphoid, cholera and — though less commonly — Guinea worm and various types of fluke. Although poliomyelitis is now uncommon in the UK, it is still a risk in many countries throughout the world. Few UK citizens below the age of fifty are now unprotected, but immunity may need to be boosted for travel to areas of higher risk. Hepatitis A in children is often a fairly mild or even subclinical illness, but in adults it is usually more debilitating. Jaundice is likely, though not inevitable, and the illness may last for many weeks, but mortality is not high. Typhoid presents initially as a fever, though eventually diarrhoea and more widespread systemic disease may occur. Typhoid is less likely to affect Western travellers than is hepatitis A. Most of the cases occurring originate from travellers to the Indian subcontinent, but Africa and parts of South America also carry an increased risk of typhoid. Cholera is even less likely in Western travellers. It occurs principally in (and is more likely to lead to serious morbidity or to mortality in) populations with poor socio-economic status, in poor nutritional condition and/or having prior ill health.

Immersion in fresh (non-salty) water may result in infection with schistosomiasis, particularly in African countries and some parts of the Far East. Probably the largest single source of schistosomiasis for UK travellers is swimming in Lake Malawi. The intermediate host of the infection is a freshwater snail. Penetration of intact skin occurs and there may be an initial skin reaction ('swimmer's itch') at the site of entry of the parasites. There may also, at a later stage, be a pyrexial illness. The intestinal form of the disease leads to a dysenteric type of illness, with severe inflammation of the wall of the large intestine and complications including ulceration, bleeding and pseudo-polyp formation. The urinary tract form of the disease leads to inflammation of the bladder wall with haematuria, obstruction, renal damage and possible malignant change.

Travellers' diarrhoea

This is a very common experience for travellers from developed countries to less developed countries, or to countries with lower standards of food and general hygiene. In some countries it occurs in up to fifty per cent or more of travellers (Farthing, 1994). It may occur in various degrees of severity ranging from a minor outburst lasting 24 hours or less, to a chronic debilitating problem or a severe or even life-threatening illness. In its milder form it may simply represent the reaction of the gut as it adjusts to a new type of bacterial population or to changes in diet. Infection may also occur with a wide variety of pathogenic organisms including strains of E coli, Salmonellas, Shigellas, Campylobacter, viruses such as rotavirus, and protozoa such as cryptosporidium, amoeba and giardia. As with many other infections, the very young, the very old and those whose immune system is compromised by illness are more at risk of developing diarrhoea. Also at increased risk are those whose gastric acid output is reduced by medication such as H_2 antagonists (for example cimetidine, ranitidine), antacids, or proton pump inhibitors (for example omeprazole, lansoprazole).

Prevention of travellers' diarrhoea

This depends on the avoidance of sources of infection and could be summarised in the following rules.

1 Drinking water must be boiled (it has been claimed that water should be boiled for five to ten minutes, but recent research suggests that simply bringing to the boil may be adequate) or treated with chlorine-releasing tablets or (preferably) iodine (add four to six drops of two per cent tincture of iodine to one litre of water and leave to stand for twenty minutes before drinking). Any visible detritus should first be filtered (even if only through a few folds of a clean handkerchief), preferably through a purifying filter. Bottled water and other drinks are usually safe to drink provided that the seal is unbroken.
2 Ice must not be added to drinks as it may have been made from contaminated water. The alcohol content of drinks is not high enough to kill pathogenic organisms.
3 Peel fruit before eating, and salads should be avoided.

4   Food that is freshly cooked at a high temperature and brought straight to the table is usually safe to eat, but reheated food or food laid out in a buffet may not be.

5   Seafood, especially molluscs such as mussels, must be regarded with suspicion.

6   Dairy products such as milk (unless boiled), butter, cheese and ice-cream should be avoided, as milk is unlikely to have been pasteurised.

7   Food from street stalls or vendors, or from any source open to flies, should be avoided.

8   An often-quoted piece of advice is: 'Boil it, cook it, peel it or throw it away!'

Treatment of travellers' diarrhoea

Rehydration therapy

This is the initial treatment and is often the only treatment needed. A solution of salt and sugar may be prepared using purified or bottled water with a tablespoon of sugar and half a teaspoon of salt to each pint. The recipe often suggested by aid agencies abroad is a palmful of sugar and a three-finger pinch of salt to half a litre of water. However, travellers may find it more convenient to carry ready-prepared sachets such as Dioralyte and Rehidrat, or to buy similar, locally-made preparations, usually very cheaply. The solution should be taken liberally, but if vomiting occurs smaller volumes taken more frequently are advisable. It is not always necessary to stop eating, but it may be wise to confine eating to easily absorbed carbohydrate such as white bread, boiled rice and boiled potatoes.

Antidiarrhoeal drugs

These include drugs such as diphenoxylate/atropine (Lomotil) and loperamide (Imodium). They help to slow down stool frequency, though they do not cure the diarrhoea. They are very useful for travellers as it is not easy to respond to repeated calls to stool during, for example, a prolonged road or rail journey or in a tent in sub-zero temperatures.

Antibacterial drugs

This type of drug should be used if diarrhoea is accompanied by systemic illness, for example pyrexia, or if it becomes severe or prolonged beyond about 48 hours. It is not usually possible to obtain a stool culture or to ascertain from clinical features the nature of the infecting organism, and the use of broad spectrum antibacterials such as quinolones, for example ciprofloxacin (Ciproxin), is therefore recommended. An alternative choice would be co-trimoxazole. A standard course of five days may be followed but there is some evidence that a single dose of 500 mg of ciprofloxacin may be effective in many cases. Travellers at particular risk of diarrhoea because of the nature of their journey may be given supplies of antibacterial drugs together with written instructions for their use. Prophylactic use of antibacterial drugs is a little more controversial, but there may be an argument for giving prophylaxis to travellers going on short visits to areas of high risk, who cannot afford the risk of illness because of the important nature of their visit.

Chronic diarrhoea

Less dramatic but more prolonged diarrhoea may be caused by infection with amoeba or giardia. In such instances, there may be passage of blood and, in the case of giardia, foul-smelling flatus or eructation of wind. Treatment with metronidazole or tinidazole is usually effective.

Soil

Tetanus

This is present worldwide as spores in soil, particularly when contaminated by animal droppings. Infection enters through minute and sometimes invisible breaches in the skin surface. Even where high-quality intensive care is available mortality is still high.

Hookworm

Larvae usually enter through intact skin on the feet from soil contaminated with human faeces. The possibility of infection is widespread and is increased by walking barefoot or by wearing inadequately protective footwear such a flip-flops. Adult hookworms colonise the small intestine where they feed on blood, causing anaemia which may be profound in the case of heavy infestation.

Strongyloides

This is an intestinal worm that may also be acquired by penetration of the skin of the feet. Although it may apparently be symptomless, it can also lead to prolonged or even lifelong infestation, with abdominal symptoms and sometimes with allergic manifestations, including eosinophilia in peripheral blood.

Insects

Apart from the irritation caused by bites and, in some people, allergic reactions to bites, there are many diseases that are transmitted from insects to humans. Measures for avoiding insect bites will be discussed in detail in *Chapter 5* on malaria.

Mosquitoes

Malaria

Malaria is the most important of tropical diseases in terms of widespread morbidity and mortality. It is present in many tropical and subtropical parts of the world and is transmitted to humans by bites from the female anopheline mosquito. It has also been reported as occurring from transfusion of infected blood, or other blood-borne transmission such as the re-use of needles. Although the great majority of infections occur in the tropics and sub-tropics, malaria has been known to occur in temperate countries from the bites of mosquitoes transported there in aircraft.

Malaria will be discussed in more detail in *Chapter 5*. Its prevention depends on the avoidance of mosquito bites, though prophylactic drugs have an important part to play. There is as yet no effective vaccine against malaria.

Dengue fever

Initially, dengue is a flu-like illness. It is characterised by headaches and severe muscular pains ('break-bone fever'), and a rash often occurs. In acute cases, especially in children, a severe haemorrhagic form of the disease may occur. Dengue fever is acquired from the bites of Aedes mosquitoes, and occurs in the tropical areas of Asia, Africa, Central and South America. There is no specific treatment and no vaccine or other preventive measure, apart from avoidance of mosquito bites.

Filariasis

Filariasis is an infestation by worms that inhabit lymphatic tissue. It occurs in Asia, Africa, South America and Oceania and may cause episodes of fever, pain and oedema with, eventually, chronic and sometimes enormous oedema of the limbs or genitalia (that is, elephantiasis). It is acquired by the transmission of microfilariae from the bites of infected culicine or anopheline mosquitoes which, depending on the variety of filaria and the species of mosquito, may bite by day or night.

Filariasis is treated with diethylcarbamazine but apart from the avoidance of bites there is no other method of prophylaxis.

Yellow fever

This, like dengue fever, is an arborvirus (arthropod-borne, that is, insect-borne virus) infection. It is found in African and Central/South American countries close to the Equator where there are Aedes mosquitoes that are capable of transmitting it to humans. It originates in jungle areas where it is acquired by mosquitoes from monkeys and passed on to humans when they are bitten by infected mosquitoes. In urban areas it can then be transmitted from one infected human to another, also by means of mosquito bites. The symptoms of fever, headache, muscle pains, abdominal pain and vomiting may be followed by bleeding and hepatic or renal failure.

Fortunately, vaccination is very effective and lasts for ten years. A current International Certificate of Vaccination is required for entry to many countries where the disease is found, and vaccination is advisable for all such countries even when it is not a statutory requirement. Some countries that do not have the disease may have mosquitoes capable of transmitting it. These countries may demand an International Certificate from travellers entering from a country where yellow fever exists.

Japanese encephalitis

This is another arborvirus infection occurring in South and South-

East Asia, and that is transmitted to humans by the bites of culicine mosquitoes. The animal carriers of this infection are domestic/farm animals, particularly pigs. The mosquito vectors breed in standing water, especially in rice paddies. The infection is therefore most likely to be acquired in rural, rice-growing areas in the wet season in travellers who spend a prolonged period (that is, a month or more) in such an environment. The illness is severe, with fever which may lead to coma, meningitis, encephalitis and paralysis. There is a considerable mortality rate from the disease, which tends to be particularly severe in children.

Vaccination is effective but the vaccine is not licensed in the UK and must be obtained on a named patient basis. Travellers fitting the above profile should be offered the vaccine, and anti-mosquito precautions are essential.

Flies

Leishmaniasis

This is a disease transmitted by the bites of Phlebotomus sandflies. Its cutaneous form, characterised by skin nodules which often ulcerate, is found in Africa, Mediterranean countries, the Middle East and Central and South America. The mucosal form, which may cause severe ulceration around the nose and mouth, is found in Central and South America. The visceral form (kala-azar) is found scattered through Africa, southern Europe, the Middle East, Asia and Central and South America. It causes fever, anaemia, weight loss, and enlargement — often massive — of the liver and spleen.

The only means of avoiding infection, which in the case of visceral leishmaniasis is uncommon among travellers, is by avoiding sandfly bites. The flies bite both at dusk and dawn, and the use of clothing that covers exposed skin, insect repellents containing DEET and sleeping under a net impregnated with the insecticide permethrin are recommended. As sandflies do not fly high, sleeping on the roof may be a good policy.

Onchocerciasis

This disease, otherwise known as river blindness, occurs in Africa and to some extent in South America. The causative worm is introduced into humans as microfilariae by the bites of blackflies.

Adult worms take up residence in the skin where they may cause a great deal of structural damage, and may affect the eyes, leading to chronic irritation and blindness.

The condition itself is treatable with ivermectin but prevention depends on avoiding bites (see above). Blackflies live near fast-flowing water, and camping near such areas should be avoided. The flies may also be attracted by wood smoke.

African trypanosomiasis (sleeping sickness)

This is acquired from the bite of the tsetse fly which is found in central parts of Africa. A chancre (lesion) at the site of the bite is followed by fever, lymphadenopathy and possibly a rash. This may be followed by disturbances of cerebral function, dementia and coma. In the more virulent rhodesiense form of the disease, the acute stage is more toxic and may be fatal before neurological damage appears. The animal reservoirs of infection are cattle or game animals, and the tsetse fly bites during the daytime.

Prevention, once again, is by avoidance of bites. Travellers on game safaris should keep their vehicle windows closed and use insecticide sprays. Insect repellents help to some extent.

Bugs, fleas, lice and ticks

South American trypanosomiasis (Chaga's disease)

This causes chronic disease of the heart or hollow digestive organs. It is transmitted by the bites of bugs which live in the walls of mud huts and emerge to bite during the night. For this reason it is uncommon in travellers unless they spend long periods in such accommodation.

Plague

This is also uncommon among travellers. It is acquired from rats or other rodents via the bites of fleas. A vaccine is available but is unlikely to be required by most travellers.

Typhus

This is a feverish, flu-like illness which may be acquired from body lice — particularly by those working with refugees, or from ticks by walkers in some tropical areas, Mediterranean countries or the Americas (Rocky Mountain spotted fever). A blackened eschar may occur at the site of the tick bite. Walkers in areas of potential risk should avoid tick bites by keeping the lower limbs covered and by regular inspection for the presence of ticks.

Tick-borne encephalitis

This may be acquired in northern, central or eastern Europe from the bites of ticks. Walkers, or those intending to work in forests, are most at risk. After a flu-like illness there may be meningitis, encephalitis and paralysis. A vaccine is available but it is not licensed in the UK and must be obtained on a named patient basis.

Animals

Rabies

Rabies is a virus infection of mammals which is transmitted to humans by bites, scratches or licks. Dogs are a common source of infection for humans, but almost any mammal may constitute a risk. It is easier to enumerate the countries where rabies is not a risk — currently the UK, Ireland, Norway, Sweden, Iceland, Australia, New Zealand, Antarctica, Oceania, New Guinea, Malaysia (peninsular), Taiwan and Japan. The overall level of risk to travellers is low but the maximum risk is in the Indian subcontinent. Once the disease becomes symptomatic, it is fatal to humans.

There is an effective virus for prophylaxis but post-exposure treatment with rabies vaccine is still required, even if vaccination has already been performed. Pre-exposure vaccination reduces the number of post-vaccination doses needed and buys a little time in which to obtain them. It should be offered to all travellers who are travelling to areas of risk and who will be more than 24 hours away from a reliable source of medical help and rabies vaccine, or who intend to work with animals.

Close personal contact

Although travellers' minds will be focussed on more exotic diseases, they should be aware that they will be at least as prone to common illnesses, such as upper respiratory infections and influenza, as they would be at home. In the case of influenza, the risk may be greater and may exist throughout the year, not being confined to one season as it is in the UK. Some other diseases depend for their spread on closer personal contact and for longer periods, usually by upper respiratory droplet infection. It is these diseases with which this section is mostly concerned.

Meningococcal disease

Meningococcal infection is spread by nasopharyngeal droplet infection and needs close or prolonged contact with an infected individual or carrier. Overcrowding and the sharing of living and more particularly sleeping accommodation increase the likelihood of infection with the disease. The backpacker or trekker using local-style accommodation (especially in Nepal) and the remote traveller, aid worker or teacher in sub-Saharan Africa or the Indian subcontinent are most at risk. Vaccination is now mandatory for the Haj pilgrimage to Mecca, on which large numbers of pilgrims share sleeping accommodation in tents. Amongst Western travellers, the majority of meningococcal infections occurs in the under-25 age group. The illness is usually of rapid onset and progression with fever, irritability, headache and increasing toxicity leading to neck rigidity and impaired consciousness. A petechial rash often occurs but is not always present. Typical symptoms and signs may be absent in small children. Infants may have a bulging anterior fontanelle.

The meningococcal vaccine that is currently available offers protection against both the A strain that occurs in Africa, the Indian subcontinent and elsewhere, and the C strain sometimes found in the UK. The most common strain causing illness in the UK is the B strain, against which the current vaccine is not effective.

Tuberculosis

This is a worldwide problem but, again, Africa and the Indian subcontinent are areas of particular risk. There is now an increasing risk in the Western world that is, at least in part, associated with AIDS. Unlike the rapid onset of meningococcal disease, TB has an incubation period that may last several weeks, and its clinical manifestations may vary from pulmonary disease with a cough, sputum and weight loss to abdominal or urinary tract disease, skeletal involvement, enlarged lymph nodes or widespread miliary disease. The travellers most at risk are long-stay travellers in close contact with local people. There is also a risk for immigrants in the UK who return home to visit their families, particularly in the Indian sub-continent.

The BCG vaccine — a routine vaccination for UK residents in their early teens — offers good protection. Any un-immunised tuberculin non-reactor should be given the BCG vaccine before travelling to an area of high risk, particularly for a long stay or in circumstances of close contact with local people.

Diphtheria

This is a disease that frequently involves the throat, producing a sore throat, a thick membrane on the tonsils and pharynx and possibly laryngeal involvement with stridor and hoarseness. It may also have serious toxic effects on the heart and nervous system. Diphtheria may also affect the skin, causing ulceration. It occurs in many countries, including India, and in recent years there has been a marked increase in its incidence in countries of the former Soviet Union. Travellers to such areas should be offered diphtheria vaccine, especially if they will be in close contact with local people.

Other diseases of close physical contact

Leprosy

Leprosy may occur from physical contact but droplet infection is probably a more likely means of spread. There is no means of prevention by drugs or vaccination. It is extremely uncommon in Western travellers, and no further description is required for present purposes.

Skin infections

These may occur from direct bodily contact. Impetigo, fungal infections and scabies may all occur.

Geographical distribution of travel-related diseases

In order to advise travellers about the health hazards that they are likely to encounter, it is necessary for the GP or practice nurse to have access to information about diseases and health hazards present in the countries to be visited. It is also essential to have information about the topography and climate of the destinations so as to be able to give advice about hazards from physical and climatic conditions such as heat, cold and altitude. If the adviser is also a traveller some of this information may be available from first-hand experience, but few doctors or nurses are likely to have enough experience to be able to advise about all possible destinations. Therefore, a reliable and regularly updated database, such as the Travax or Traveller computer databases, is essential for any travel clinic.

As well as considering the geographical distribution of a disease it is also necessary when advising travellers to examine the time of year when the disease is most prevalent, the areas of the country in which it is most prevalent and the mode of transmission. Often it is also necessary to know the length of stay, the type of accommodation to be used and the activities to be undertaken before advising on the level of risk to the individual traveller (see *Chapter 6*). When advising on prevention, it is important to look at factors other than immunisation and drug prophylaxis which may not be available for many diseases. Indeed, other factors are also important for those diseases for which prophylaxis *is* available, one example of this is the avoidance of mosquito and other insect bites.

Malaria

The subject of malaria will be covered in greater detail in *Chapter 5*. Malaria is present in many countries with hot climates. Central America, many northern parts of South America, Africa — virtually from the Sahara down to, but excluding, South Africa, and South and South-East Asia are the principal areas affected, but parts of the Middle East also carry a risk of malaria (see *Figure 1.1* on page 14). It is important in many cases to know which parts of a country a traveller intends to visit. Malaria may be present in some parts but not in others, or different prophylactic drugs may be needed in different areas. Countries may carry a risk of malaria in some low-lying areas, but other areas may be at a higher and therefore cooler elevation where malaria does not exist.

Figure 1.1: Malaria distribution

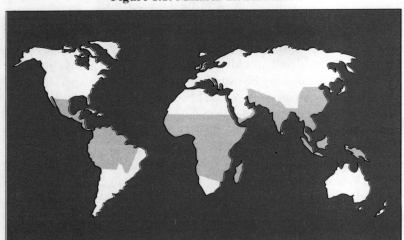

Yellow fever

Yellow fever is present throughout the northern countries of South America, and in Africa virtually from the Sahara down to, but excluding, South Africa (see *Figure 1.2* on *page 15*). In many parts of these areas, vaccination and the production of a valid vaccination certificate are compulsory as a condition of entry into the country. Other areas that are currently free of yellow fever have mosquitoes capable of spreading the disease if it were to be introduced into them. These areas include Central America, South Africa, North Africa along the Mediterranean coast, South and South-East Asia, China and parts of the Middle East. Some of these countries may require evidence of yellow fever vaccination from those entering from a country where yellow fever is endemic.

Hepatitis A

Hepatitis A is a potential hazard worldwide, but because it is spread by the faecal-oral route, it is more likely to be encountered in countries where standards of food and water hygiene, and of sewage disposal are not as high as in the UK. Those countries where there is not an increased risk of hepatitis A include northern and western Europe, Scandinavia, the USA, Canada, Australia and New Zealand (see *Figure 1.3* on *page 15*).

Figure 1.2: Yellow fever distribution

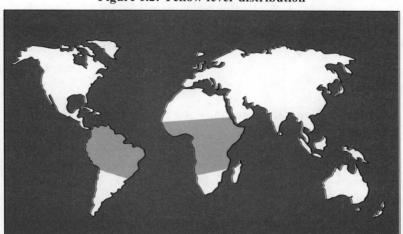

Figure 1.3: Hepatitis A distribution

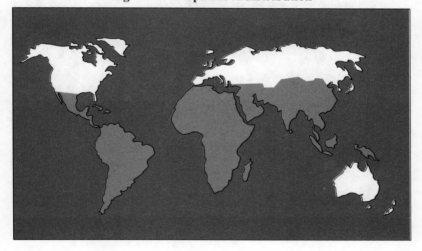

Dengue

Dengue fever is widespread in the Tropics and is generally found in Central America, northern parts of South America, the Caribbean, Africa, South-East Asia, the Pacific region and occasionally in other areas.

Poliomyelitis

As polio is also a disease spread by the faecal-oral route, similar remarks again apply.

Hepatitis B

Hepatitis B is another potentially worldwide problem but, for the traveller, the principal areas of risk are in Africa and some parts of Asia and South America (see *Figure 1.4*). Transfusion with infected blood, surgical or other procedures such as ear piercing or tattooing, intravenous drug use, and sexual contact are all potential modes of transmission.

Figure 1.4: Hepatitis B distribution

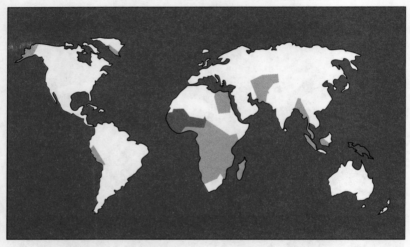

black = highest risk; light blue = high risk; white = some risk

Typhoid

Typhoid is spread by the faecal-oral route. The countries where there is not a significant risk are much the same as those given for hepatitis A, but a majority of cases seen in travellers returning to the UK originate from the Indian subcontinent (see *Figure 1.5* on *page 17*).

Figure 1.5: Typhoid distribution

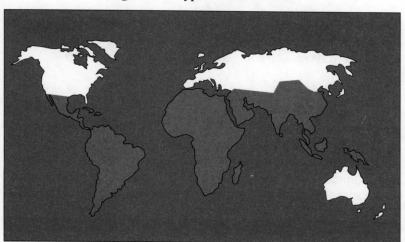

Rabies

Although there is a widespread distribution of rabies in many areas including the USA and Europe, the greatest risks exist in Asia, Africa and Central and South America. Bites or scratches from small mammals, including those of dogs and monkeys, are the means of transmission, and veterinary workers or travellers likely to come into contact with animals by reason of their itinerary or activities are at risk.

Meningococcal disease

The areas of most risk for travellers are sub-Saharan Africa, Asia (particularly India and Nepal), parts of South America, and Saudi Arabia. This disease is most likely to be a problem in the hot, dry season and in conditions when travellers are in close contact with local people, for example in their living, sleeping or working environment.

Japanese B encephalitis

This disease, despite its name, is no longer a problem in Japan but is present throughout much of Asia from Nepal and India southwards and eastwards into the Pacific region. It is most likely to occur in the wet season in rural areas among longer-term travellers.

Tick-borne encephalitis

The risk of tick-borne encephalitis is confined mainly to the forested areas of Scandinavia, central and eastern Europe. The travellers most at risk are walkers and campers.

Schistosomiasis (bilharzia)

This is found principally in Africa (where it is present in most areas except the Sahara) and in parts of South-East Asia, China and northern South America, in fresh (non-salt) water. The parasite, whose intermediate host is a species of snail, gains access by penetrating intact skin. The risk can be avoided by keeping out of water, except purified swimming pools.

Filariasis

The distribution of filariasis, acquired from mosquito bites, is similar to that of the other diseases spread by mosquitoes, such as malaria, yellow fever and dengue, though it is less prevalent in South America. Although the disease is not common in travellers, longer-term travellers are at risk.

Leishmaniasis

Cutaneous leishmaniasis occurs in the Mediterranean region, the Middle East and parts of Africa and South America, and is a potential risk for some travellers. Visceral leishmaniasis (kala azar) occurs in a similar distribution and also in India, but is not common among travellers. Sandfly bites are the means of transmission.

Trypanosomiasis

African trypanosomiasis (sleeping sickness) occurs in Central and West Africa in its gambiense variety, and in East Africa in its rhodesiense variety. It is a hazard chiefly for travellers on safari where tsetse flies may bite. American trypanosomiasis (Chaga's disease) occurs in Central and South America, but travellers are at little risk unless they are sleeping in adobe huts where the disease is spread by bites from bugs living in the walls.

Emerging and re-emerging diseases

Diseases that have made their first appearance or that, following disappearance or virtual disappearance, have reappeared within a period of one or two decades, are often referred to as emerging or re-emerging diseases.

Ever since mankind first started to travel beyond his own primitive settlements, disease has been spread by travel. In early history there were the biblical plagues associated with wars and conquests, and the fall of Athens following a mysterious illness possibly spread along the Athenian Empire's trade routes. Later came the bubonic plague of the Middle Ages, again spread along trade routes, while the Spanish conquistadores killed more of the people of South America by introducing smallpox than they did by means of their swords. In more recent times, colonial conquests were probably responsible for the worldwide spread of cholera.

The most notable example of an emerging disease in recent years has been HIV/AIDS. It originally emerged in Africa and the likely route of spread was to the Caribbean, the USA and from there to Europe and to most of the rest of the world. Sexual spread by both heterosexual and homosexual routes, the use of infected blood and blood products and needle-sharing during the social use of injectable drugs have all played a part, and the ease and rapidity of modern travel have also facilitated the rapid spread of HIV infection. The World Health Organization reports that at the end of 1996, 22.6 million adults and children had been infected with HIV, and that 8.4 million cases of AIDS were documented (WHO, 1997).

In 1991 cholera emerged as a health risk in Peru and reached epidemic proportions. Cholera is usually a disease of indigenous peoples and it is unusual for it to affect travellers, but cases have occurred. Some of these cases may have been associated with eating ceviche, a raw marinated fish dish, which is a well-known delicacy in Central and South America.

Hanta virus, found in the southern United States and South

America, has emerged in recent years as a cause of a frequently severe pulmonary infection. It is transmitted by contact with the urine or droppings of small rodents and is unlikely to occur in most travellers, though campers may be at risk.

Haemorrhagic fevers such as Lassa and ebola have emerged in parts of Africa. In spite of the publicity they have received they present little risk to most travellers, but the diagnosis should be considered in patients with a pyrexia of unknown origin who have recently returned from an African country that is known to have a risk of one of these diseases. Initially often associated with a sore throat, they progress rapidly to a severe illness with haemorrhagic manifestations.

With increasing travel, malaria is seen in countries in which it is not endemic. Most cases are seen in travellers returning from malarial areas, but occasional cases of 'airport malaria' have been reported in individuals who have not travelled, presumably from the bites of mosquitoes that have been carried back in aircraft cabins.

For some years prior to the break-up of the Soviet Union diphtheria had not been present to any appreciable extent but, as newly-formed republics struggled with the problems resulting from the loss of central government structures and financial assistance, public health and vaccination programmes largely collapsed, and the disease has since begun to reappear in many former Soviet Union countries.

Tuberculosis provides an example of another disease that has re-emerged in many industrialised, as well as developing countries in association with poverty, overcrowding and/or HIV/AIDS.

2

Travel-related disease — environmental and climatic hazards

Effects of heat and sun

Many travellers go abroad with the express intention of finding a hot sunny climate. Apart from the fact that hot climates carry a higher risk of diseases (see *Chapter 1*), the effects of heat and sunlight also put the traveller, particularly the unacclimatised traveller, at risk.

Heat

Prickly heat is a rash consisting of small and intensely itchy and irritating papules or vesicles more likely to be found on the upper part of the body. It is caused by excessive sweating with obstruction of sweat ducts so that the sweat cannot escape. It may be avoided to some extent by keeping cool and by wearing cool and loose-fitting clothing. The symptoms, which may drive the sufferer almost to distraction, may be relieved by cool showers and the use of simple remedies such as calamine lotion.

Heat exhaustion is the result of excessive sweating with loss of salt and water. It may cause weakness, dizziness, lethargy, disorientation or collapse due to lowering of the blood pressure. The mouth feels dry and urine output is reduced, the urine being darker in colour. Muscle cramps may occur. The condition may be avoided by an adequate fluid intake — a good guide to its adequacy being the passage of normal volumes of light-coloured urine. At least in the early stages of acclimatisation to heat, a little extra salt in the food may be needed but salt tablets as such are usually unnecessary. Treatment consists of fluid replacement with the addition of a small quantity of salt (for example, half a teaspoonful per litre).

Heat hyperpyrexia — or heat stroke — is a serious medical emergency in which the body's cooling mechanism fails to work and sweating ceases. Body temperature rises dramatically and may reach extremely high levels, and the skin surface feels hot and dry. Headache, confusion and ultimately coma may follow and, unless external cooling is carried out, death may occur within a short time.

Sunlight

In addition to the visible spectrum of light, sunlight provides ultraviolet (UV) radiation which is divided into three categories according to its wavelength. Of these, UVC is potentially the most penetrating and harmful type of UV radiation, but this is absorbed by ozone in the atmosphere. Where the ozone layer has become depleted, more of this harmful radiation will penetrate to the Earth's surface. UVB is less damaging, producing tanning of the skin but with a tendency to burn before tanning occurs. Repeated exposure to UVB causes ageing of the skin and an increased risk of skin cancer. UVA is again less harmful, tending to tan before burning, but it may also cause ageing and predispose to skin cancer. Tanning by using a UVA sunbed does not offer protection against exposure to sun, and burning from UVA will still occur after using a sunbed.

Exposure of the skin to strong sunlight, especially in fair-skinned individuals and especially in the middle of the day for all skin types, should be avoided in order to limit the risks of burning in the short term and excessive ageing and skin cancer in the longer term. Exposure, when it does occur, should be gradual, beginning with no more than twenty minutes on the first day and increasing slowly, avoiding the middle hours of the day when UV radiation is at its strongest. An effective sun screen with a high protection factor should be used, and a sun hat that covers the ears is advisable. These measures are even more important in children. It should not be forgotten that sunburn does not only occur when sunbathing but is equally likely to occur during sightseeing and other activities. The effects of UV radiation are increased by proximity to sea or other stretches of water, sand or snow due to the consequent reflection of UV radiation. It is perhaps surprising to some to learn that significant exposure to UV radiation sufficient to cause burning may occur in the presence of cloud cover. The Australian motto, 'slip, slop, slap' sums up the precautions needed to avoid UV exposure: 'Slip on a shirt, slop on some cream and slap on a hat.'

Effects of cold

Cold may cause problems in two ways. There may be localised effects on the tissues, or general effects due to lowering of body temperature.

Frostbite

Peripheral parts of the body, such as the fingers, toes, nose and ears, are most likely to be affected by frostbite. Frostnip is the name sometimes given to less severe damage when no loss of tissue occurs. Numbness of the affected tissues occurs and complete recovery of sensation may take some weeks. True frostbite occurs when spasm of small blood vessels, due to cold exposure, cuts off the circulation to the peripheries. Further damage occurs as ice crystals form within the cells and disrupt their structure. The tissues affected are cold, white and feel hard and 'dead' to the touch. The risk of frostbite is increased by inadequate clothing, loss of equipment such as gloves, wind chill, wetness, hypothermia, constricting clothing or footwear around a limb, exhaustion and injury. Eventually, following rewarming, a line of demarcation forms and the tissues beyond it become gangrenous, though the extent of tissue loss is often less than initial appearances would predict.

Hypothermia

Immersion in cold water or exposure to cold climatic conditions may cause the body core temperature to fall to such an extent that function becomes impaired. Predisposing factors include inadequate clothing, wetness, wind chill, exhaustion, lack of food, and injury. The symptoms of hypothermia comprise violent shivering, clumsiness and lack of co-ordination, lethargy and confusion. As the temperature falls further, shivering stops and loss of consciousness occurs. The very young, the very old and the physically unfit are more prone to hypothermia. Some drugs, for example phenothiazine tranquillisers and alcohol, predispose to hypothermia. The members of a party travelling in conditions in which hypothermia could occur should be encouraged to use the 'buddy system' and keep a watch on each other for early signs of hypothermia. Established hypothermia is an emergency which could result in death.

Effects of high altitude

High altitude travel is no longer the exclusive province of the serious mountaineer. Many holidaymakers now take trekking holidays that may take them as high as 5,500 metres (17,000 feet). It is easy, even for elderly travellers, to reach over 3,500 metres (12,000 feet) on tours to, for example, South America. The threshold for altitude problems to occur is usually about 3,000 metres (10,000 feet), though problems sometimes occur at altitudes lower than this. Youth and fitness are no protection from these problems and, indeed, the young and fit appear to be more prone to them. This may perhaps be because the young and fit are more likely to press ahead more rapidly, even if early signs of altitude problems occur. Overexertion, dehydration and too rapid an ascent are all likely to increase the risk of altitude problems. The rate of ascent on foot can usually be controlled so as to avoid problems, but some itineraries include arrival at altitudes of over 3,000 metres by road or air, for example flying into the Himalayas in Nepal for trekking or sightseeing, or flying or travelling by road or train into the Andes in Peru for similar types of holiday. In this sort of circumstance altitude problems become more likely because gradual acclimatisation is not possible. Brief excursions to high altitude followed by descent, as may occur when skiing, cause no more than transient symptoms. It is when the individual stays and sleeps at over 3,000 metres that problems tend to occur.

As altitude increases, atmospheric pressure falls. Therefore there is a lower pressure driving oxygen into the blood in the pulmonary alveoli, even though the oxygen concentration in the inspired air is still as great as it is at sea level. At about 5,500 metres (17,000 feet) the atmospheric pressure is only fifty per cent of the sea level pressure. On the summit of Everest, at over 8,800 metres (29,000 feet), pressure is only one third of that at sea level. Permanent human habitation does not occur above about 5,500 metres (17,000 feet). Because oxygen pressure in the atmosphere — and therefore in the inspired air — is reduced as altitude increases, the amount of oxygen taken up by haemoglobin in the lungs is reduced. Because of the properties of haemoglobin, this reduction in oxygen uptake does not occur to a significant extent until an altitude of about 3,000 metres (10,000 feet) is reached. Above this altitude it is necessary to acclimatise gradually by ascending relatively slowly. The 'rules of three' are:

- above 3,000 metres
- no more than 300 metres of net height gain per day
- rest at the same altitude every third day.

What seems to be important is the sleeping altitude: more than 300 metres may be gained during the day provided the net gain from one sleeping place to the next is not significantly more than 300 metres.

The following problems associated with high altitude travel are all produced by hypoxia (that is, lower than normal levels of oxygen in the blood). Some individuals acclimatise more easily than others but, unfortunately, previous successful exposure to high altitude does not guarantee that problems will not occur.

Acute mountain sickness (AMS)

Acute mountain sickness is the most common form of altitude problem. Typical symptoms include tiredness, lethargy, nausea, loss of appetite, headaches, dizziness and sleep disturbance. Periodic breathing (Cheyne-Stokes) may occur during sleep and may be alarming for the sufferers and/or any companions. Those affected should stay at the same altitude for 24 hours before ascending higher, by which time symptoms will usually have settled. If improvement does not occur, or the symptoms become worse, sufferers should descend to a level at which the symptoms disappear. Acetazolamide (Diamox), in a daily dose of 250 mg, may help acclimatisation by stimulating respiration due to its effect on carbonic acid levels in the body. This drug is useful in the treatment of those who have had previous acclimatisation problems, or whose itinerary does not allow the kind of gradual height gain outlined above because of the lie of the land. It may also be used to treat symptoms of AMS. Its chief side effect is peripheral tingling and it also has a mild diuretic effect.

The following complications of high altitude are much less likely to occur, but are potentially fatal unless prompt and effective action is taken.

High altitude pulmonary oedema (HAPE)

HAPE appears to be caused by leaking of blood vessels in the lungs, and raised pulmonary artery pressure due to hypoxia. The symptoms are similar to those of pulmonary oedema from other causes and include breathlessness, a cough and the production of frothy white, or eventually pink (blood stained), sputum. It is much less common than AMS, but it is important to recognise it and take the necessary action as otherwise it will probably be fatal. Breathlessness is a common experience at high altitude but it will usually cease after a short period of rest. The earliest sign of HAPE is most commonly breathlessness that does not settle rapidly on resting and, if this occurs, it is not advisable to wait for other symptoms, such as a cough, to confirm the diagnosis. Immediately the condition is suspected, a descent of at least 300 metres or further is vital, until HAPE symptoms disappear. However inconvenient this may be, descent should take place without delay — even during the night — if a fatal outcome is to be avoided. Giving oxygen, where available, and a 10 mg capsule of nifedipine (bitten for buccal absorption) followed by 20 mg three times a day (eight-hourly), are useful adjuncts but should not take the place of descent. The use of a pressurised bag enclosing the patient (— the pressure is maintained by pumping) is also useful and can relieve symptoms dramatically, but it should be used while arranging descent and not instead of it. Diuretics, such as frusemide, are not useful. The causes of HAPE are different from the pulmonary oedema occurring in other conditions, and the use of diuretics may add to an already existing problem of dehydration.

High altitude cerebral oedema (HACE)

HACE appears to be caused by leaking blood vessels and an increase in cerebral blood flow due to hypoxia. Symptoms may initially resemble those of AMS, with lethargy, headache and dizziness, but progression to lack of co-ordination, drowsiness and coma soon occurs. Fits may occur, and a variety of abnormal neurological signs may appear. Once consciousness is lost death is usually not far distant and it is necessary to act quickly and preferably at a much earlier stage. The headache is more severe and persistent than that of AMS, is not relieved by simple analgesics and is likely to be made worse rather than better by lying down. A headache of this type, or lack of co-ordination in walking or simple manual tasks should trigger prompt action. As with HAPE, early and rapid descent is essential. Again, the pressurised bag may help, and a powerful steroid such as dexamethasone (8 mg at once and 4 mg every six hours) may be used as for cerebral oedema from other causes.

Dehydration due to high altitude

At high altitude the pressure of water vapour in the atmosphere is very low. This results in increased loss of water vapour from the lungs, which is further prompted by increased ventilation of the lungs due to both hypoxia and exertion. Exertion also leads to increased water loss from sweating. A fluid intake of several litres a day may be needed at very high altitude, a good guide to adequate intake being the regular passage of light-coloured urine. For many travellers, water and other drinks may be readily available and should be taken frequently. For members of climbing expeditions above the snow line, the only source of water is to melt snow, which consumes both time and precious fuel. In fact, some degree of dehydration is common in these conditions. Dehydration predisposes to altitude problems and to an increased tendency for blood to clot, as well as being a problem in its own right. Its symptoms, which may include not only a dry mouth and thirst but also lethargy, drowsiness and unsteadiness, may easily be confused with those of AMS or hypothermia.

Blood clotting

Exposure to high altitude causes an increase in the number of red cells in the blood, though this may not occur to any appreciable extent unless the stay at altitude is longer than about two or three weeks. This effect causes an increase in the ability of the blood to coagulate, which may be further increased by dehydration. These effects are more likely to occur in older travellers at altitude, and also in those with other predisposing factors such as taking oral contraceptives. Deep vein thromboses and/or pulmonary emboli may result.

Respiratory problems

As a result of the low atmospheric pressure of water vapour at high altitude, the mucous membranes of the upper respiratory tract become dry. This increases the incidence of such symptoms as a sore throat and cough, and there is then an increased likelihood of the infection descending lower into the respiratory tract and causing bronchitis or even pneumonia. There is no direct effect of altitude on asthma. Many asthmatics may benefit from the absence of their allergens in the high altitude environment, though some may be adversely affected by the effects of exertion and breathing cold air.

Problems associated with the mode of travel

Air travel

The advent of comparatively cheap and affordable air travel has revolutionised world travel, making journeys abroad possible for vastly increased numbers of people. In 1995, 1.4 billion passengers travelled by air (Office of National Statistics, 1995). Although air travel is now a commonplace feature of many holidays, it does carry with it potential hazards.

Reduced atmospheric pressure

As height above sea level increases, air pressure decreases. At about 5,500 metres (17,000 feet) atmospheric pressure is half that at sea level and on top of Everest, at around 8, 800 metres (29,000 feet), it is only one third of the sea level pressure. Commercial aircraft fly at altitudes much higher than the summit of Everest, at which their passengers would not survive without pressurisation of the aircraft.

Oxygen enters the blood inside the lungs and is bound to haemoglobin for distribution around the body. This uptake of oxygen depends on the presence of an adequate atmospheric pressure driving it into the blood to combine with haemoglobin. With small decreases in atmospheric pressure the amount of oxygen entering the blood is not affected, but as pressure falls lower, oxygenation of haemoglobin begins to decrease. If this process occurs gradually some degree of acclimatisation to lower atmospheric pressure does occur, though humans do not seem able to live permanently without damage above about 5,500 metres (17,000 feet). If atmospheric pressure, and therefore oxygenation, are reduced suddenly then severe hypoxic symptoms occur and death will follow if the reduction is a large one.

Commercial aircraft are pressurised to a degree equivalent to an altitude of about 1,500 to 2,500 metres (5,000 to 8,000 feet). In a normal, healthy individual, this is a level at which no reduction in oxygenation will take place. To pressurise an aircraft to sea-level pressures would increase its weight to such a degree that its load-carrying capacity, or even its ability to take off at all, would be greatly restricted. The reduced atmospheric and thus alveolar oxygen pressure in an aircraft cabin will not cause problems, unless an individual's oxygenation at sea level is grossly impaired due to severe cardiac or respiratory disease (for example severe COPD) and he or she is functioning on the very edge of cardio-respiratory reserves. A good guide would perhaps be that if an individual is too dyspnoeic to climb a flight of twelve domestic stairs or to walk more than fifty metres on level ground, he or she may have problems with oxygenation during a flight. It may, of course, be possible for such a person to fly using supplemental in-flight oxygen, but such a request would have to be made in advance at the time of booking. The other group of travellers who may have problems due to lower cabin pressures are those with sickle-cell disease, in whom a relatively small degree of hypoxia may precipitate a crisis. For this reason, flying soon after a sickle-cell crisis is not to be advised.

Changes in air pressure during take-off and landing may cause discomfort, and sometimes severe pain in the ears or paranasal sinuses, particularly if the individual has, or has recently had, an upper respiratory tract infection or has chronic upper respiratory problems or allergies. The Eustachian tube connects the middle ear cavity to the nasopharynx, and the ostia of the sinuses connect them to the nasal passages. The passage of air through these orifices allows the air pressure in the middle ear or sinuses to become equal to that of the atmosphere if the atmospheric pressure changes. If, however, access to the middle ear or sinuses is blocked by mucosal oedema, or any other form of obstruction, this equalisation of pressure cannot take place. In the case of the ear, middle-ear pressure would become higher than that of the surrounding atmosphere during take-off and lower during landing, with resultant distortion of the eardrum, and pain. The problem tends to be worse during landing as the structure of the Eustachian tube makes it more difficult for air to gain access to a middle-ear cavity at a lower pressure, than it is for air to escape from a middle-ear cavity at a higher pressure than its surroundings. Similar problems occur with the sinuses, and may result in severe frontal or maxillary sinus pain.

Manoeuvres to aid ventilation of the Eustachian tubes include sucking sweets, swallowing hard, swallowing with the nose pinched, and performing a Valsalva manoeuvre with the nose pinched. Sometimes a yawn may have the desired effect and, in children, crying caused by the discomfort often ventilates the eusatchian tubes and relieves the situation.

Other in-flight problems

Cabin air is regularly extracted and partially replaced with external atmospheric air and partially re-circulated. It is filtered, but humidity is not maintained at normal levels. To do so would require equipment which, once again, would add so much to the weight of the aircraft as to make it commercially non-viable. As a result, air in the aircraft cabin is very dry and evaporation takes place from the upper and lower respiratory passages. The main effect of this is that the individual easily becomes dehydrated and a high fluid intake is necessary. Alcohol, although freely available on aircraft, should not be taken, especially on long flights as it is a diuretic and adds to the problem of dehydration. Sparkling drinks may also cause discomfort due to expansion of gas in the gastrointestinal tract.

Dehydration may increase confusion in elderly passengers, or cause problems with their already reduced renal function. It will also increase the tendency of those immobilised in aircraft seats, particularly the elderly or those with other predisposing problems, to have lower limb venous thromboses. Small children are also more prone to dehydration.

The drying out of the mucous membranes of the respiratory tract may produce an irritating cough, exacerbate asthma, or render an individual more prone to acquiring upper respiratory tract infections from fellow travellers. These effects are likely to be exacerbated by proximity to the smoking area of the cabin. The front portion of the aircraft has better air quality than the back as well as being further from smokers, which may influence the choice of seats for those with respiratory problems.

Except in the more expensive accommodation, aircraft seats are somewhat confined and cramped. Prolonged immobility in such seats may cause considerable stiffness in elderly or arthritic travellers. Elderly or pregnant travellers, those who become dehydrated during flight, or those with a predisposition to thrombo-embolic disease may suffer lower limb thrombosis. It is important for all long-haul air travellers, but especially for those at particular risk, such as the groups mentioned above, to book aisle seats and to leave their seats at frequent intervals and walk along the aircraft, for example to the toilet — whether they feel the need to use it or not. When in their seats these travellers should, at intervals of perhaps half an hour, systematically put their lower limbs through a series of movements which give as full a range of movement as possible to all the joints.

Contra-indications to flying

The following list indicates the types of problem that airlines would consider as being contra-indications to travelling by air. Many of the surgical contra-indications are related to the risk of the expansion of pockets of air that may be retained in body cavities following surgery, and many of the other contra-indications are related to problems of hypoxia, bleeding or clotting. Orthopaedic problems relate chiefly to the possibility of the swelling of a limb encased in plaster of Paris. In neonates expansion of alveoli may be incomplete, and hypoxia may result from even a small drop in atmospheric pressure. The contra-indications to flying include:

- **surgical**
  - abdominal, intracranial or thoracic surgery in the last ten days
  - gastrointestinal bleed in the last ten days
- **medical**
  - myocardial infarction in the last ten days
  - uncontrolled cardiac failure
  - active thromboembolic disease
  - stroke in the last ten days (including subarachoid haemorrhage)
  - epileptic attack in the last 24 hours
  - Hb less than 7.5 g/dl
  - active sickling in the last ten days
- **ear, nose and throat**
  - active otitis media
  - middle-ear surgery in the last ten days
  - tonsillectomy in the last seven days
  - wired jaw (unless carrying wire cutters)
- **eyes**
  - penetrating injury in the last seven days
  - intraocular surgery in the last seven days
- **orthopaedic and traumatic**
  - limb in plaster of Paris (unless plaster is bivalved)
- **paediatric**
  - neonates in the first 48 hours of life
- **obstetric**
  - after 34th week of pregnancy
  - after 28th week without a medical certificate
- **psychiatric**
  - serious or psychotic mental illness (unless carrying

appropriate medication and accompanied by someone competent to administer it).

Jet lag

When travellers cross several time zones, their bodily and mental rhythms will be out of step with local time. Such factors as meal times and light or darkness will conflict with the messages that they receive from a diurnal rhythm adjusted to the time at home. This may lead to difficulty in sleeping, tiredness, irritability, poor appetite and lack of concentration. The effect is worse when travelling eastwards as it is harder for the body's diurnal rhythms to adjust to a shorter day, than to a longer day when travelling westwards. The best way of dealing with the problem is to adjust as quickly as possible to the local time schedule of eating and sleeping, avoiding the temptation to 'crash out' during local daytime. A dose of a hypnotic drug, such as zopiclone (Zimovane) for a night or two, may help to achieve this. It is advisable to postpone important meetings or decisions for at least 24 hours after a long flight in order to allow the body and mind to readjust to a new diurnal rhythm.

Sea travel

Travel in small boats may be associated with problems of motion sickness, cramped or unhygienic conditions, and the hazards of drowning, near-drowning and immersion hypothermia. At the other end of the spectrum, travel on cruise ships carries its own hazards — of too much food, alcohol or sun, and ill-advised sexual encounters. Motion sickness may also occur, as may trauma from falling down companion-ways which is often due to over-indulgence in alcohol.

Motion sickness

A discrepancy in the signals relevant to movement received by the eyes and the other sensory organs such as the labyrinths, is thought to be responsible for motion sickness. Looking ahead rather than sideways from a moving ship or a vehicle, and occupation of the mind and senses with some task are beneficial, but reading may exacerbate the problem. Lying horizontal is also often helpful, but an over-stuffy atmosphere and sickly smells are counter-productive.

Treatment by drugs involves the use of antihistamines such as promethazine (Phenergan), or similar drugs, for example cyclizine (Marzine), prochlorperazine (Stemetil) or cinnarizine (Stugeron). Even more effective is hyoscine, the most convenient and efficacious way of taking it being in the form of transdermal patches (Scopoderm).

Overland travel

Here one of the principal hazards that occurs is that of road traffic accidents. Traffic regulations are less rigid, or less well-observed in many countries than they are in the UK, and vehicles and tyres are often less well-maintained. Other problems encountered are lack of sleep, poor hygiene including food, water, sanitation and personal hygiene, and the close proximity of fellow travellers, their diseases and sometimes their animals, and other allergens. Conditions are very often hot and dusty, leading to the problems of dehydration (especially in the presence of diarrhoea or vomiting) and respiratory infections. Cramped conditions and prolonged immobility add to the problems.

Backpacking

Backpackers are usually young and travelling on a tight budget. The very nature of their travelling leaves them wide open to the problems of poor food and water hygiene, inadequate sanitation, and close contact with local people and animals. Accommodation is likely to be of a low standard of comfort and hygiene with fleas, lice, mosquitoes and other insects being in close attendance. Sexual encounters with other travellers or with local people carry a risk of sexually-transmitted diseases, including HIV and hepatitis B.

Backpackers need to be advised about a much wider range of hazards than do most package holidaymakers or five-star travellers, in view of their greater exposure to risks and the longer periods of time for which they are exposed to them.

3

Problems of specific groups of travellers

Groups of travellers

Children

Pre-travel precautions

It is wise to make sure that babies have had at least their primary immunisations against polio, tetanus and diphtheria before taking them abroad. Typhoid vaccine may be given to children as young as six to twelve months, though the younger ones may have a pyrexial reaction. However, the oral typhoid vaccine is not licensed for children under the age of six years. Yellow fever vaccine is not suitable for children under the age of nine months because there is an increased risk of encephalitis occurring. Children under the age of eighteen months do not achieve as good an antibody response as do older children to capsular polysaccharide vaccines such as typhoid Vi and meningococcal vaccines. However, partial protection may be obtained by their use which is advisable, particularly in the case of the meningococcal vaccine, as young children are at greater risk of infection than adults. Hepatitis A vaccine may be given to babies of six months and possibly younger, but there is some debate about whether it is really needed. Hepatitis A is very often a mild or even subclinical illness in young children that will be followed by immunity, and some would recommend withholding the vaccine on these grounds. This should be discussed with the parents before a decision is reached. If Japanese encephalitis is a distinct risk young children may be vaccinated as they are at increased risk of severe illness from it.

Anti-malarial precautions are important for children. No drug prophylaxis is recommended for babies of under six weeks of age, but chloroquine or chloroquine plus proguanil may be given from that age upwards. Suitable dosages are given in the *British National Formulary* (Mehta, 1998), and will be discussed further in *Chapter 5*. The use of mefloquine is not recommended for children of under

15 kilograms in weight, and chloroquine and proguanil should be used for chloroquine-resistant malaria. Maloprim is not frequently used in the UK but may be used for children over the age of one year. Doxycycline is not suitable for use in treating children because of the tetracycline effect on bones and teeth.

Anti-mosquito precautions are most important for children, and become crucial if they are unable, by reason of age or size, to take an appropriate anti-malarial drug. Nets over beds, cots and even prams, skin covering and insect repellents will greatly reduce the risk of malaria between dusk and dawn. Children are at a greater risk than are adults from dengue and Japanese encephalitis in countries where these diseases exist. Dengue and Japanese encephalitis are also spread by mosquitoes, as is yellow fever. Those children too young to receive yellow fever vaccine, if they must be taken to an area of risk, must be protected against mosquitoes. It is wise always to protect young children against flies and mosquitoes during daylight so as to avoid the discomfort of bites and the risk of diseases spread by daytime, biting insects.

During travel

Travel sickness is a problem with which many parents are all too familiar. It is caused by a discrepancy between what the eyes see as movement and what the body perceives as staying still, while travelling. It appears to be exacerbated by concentrating on such tasks as reading while travelling, or by looking sideways out of a moving vehicle. Drugs, such as prochlorperazine (Stemetil) or cinnarizine (Stugeron) or even antihistamines, may help to prevent or reduce symptoms, but at the cost of drowsiness or irritability.

Children with either acute or chronic upper respiratory tract problems may experience quite severe pain in their ears with air travel during take-off and even more so during landing. This is due to pressure changes in the middle ear cavity caused by Eustachian tube obstruction. Sucking, chewing or swallowing may all help to ventilate the Eustachian tubes during take-off and landing. Crying is also very effective.

Keeping young children happily occupied throughout a long journey is one of the greatest problems. An ample supply of familiar toys, books and recorded tapes, together with a few carefully concealed surprises when the former begin to pall is probably the best answer, as well as an ability in the carer to improvise games from surrounding objects and events.

Infant feeding during travel is relatively easy for the breast-fed baby. For the bottle-fed baby, a supply of water suitable for making up feeds may be difficult to obtain. Bottled mineral water is usually suitable and the airline cabin crew can usually provide a means of heating water for feeds or for warming ready-prepared feeds. For slightly older infants, jars of prepared foods are easily carried and can probably be warmed by airline staff, if necessary.

On arrival

Food and water hygiene are extremely important for the health of young children (see *Chapter 1* on sources of infection). Again, breast-fed babies are at an advantage. Water for making up feeds must be adequately purified. Prepared baby foods may not be available and suitable meals will then need to be improvised. Drinking water, fruit, sweetmeats and ice-cream are all potential sources of infection for the older child who needs to be educated about the risks and then frequently reminded of them. Children easily become dehydrated if they develop diarrhoea, and oral rehydration is of prime importance.

General hygiene is problematic with toddlers, who tend to wander around putting everything in their mouths — eating dirt, and so on. In some environments, going barefoot puts children at risk of hookworm, strongyloides and larva migrans.

Both climatic and environmental hazards need to be taken into account when children are taken travelling. They must be adequately protected from the sun by means of clothing, hats and sun-screen creams. Children are easily affected by dehydration in hot climates, and adequate fluid intake is vital. In cold environments children easily become hypothermic and must be kept warm with suitable clothing and regular food and drink. Children are also prone to altitude sickness and must not be taken too high too quickly, or pushed beyond their physical limits when ascending.

Elderly travellers

The elderly may apparently be fit and healthy and, like other sections of the population, they often wish to travel. Their fitness may, however, represent a very fine balance because many of their physiological functions deteriorate gradually with increasing age, to the point where it takes relatively little physical or mental stress to push them over the edge into abnormal function.

Mental functions

Travel, especially with a change of time zones, can be extremely disorienting, and airports in particular can be very confusing places. Elderly travellers may easily become bewildered and disoriented, and may need help and guidance through unfamiliar procedures.

Cardiorespiratory functions

The physical stresses of rushing through stations or airports carrying luggage, or the unfamiliar exertion of sightseeing trips, may either exacerbate pre-existing angina or heart failure, or unmask them for the first time. Flying is unlikely to cause problems from reduced air pressure unless cardiorespiratory functions are grossly undermined at sea level by severe heart disease or severe chronic lung disease. In general, an elderly person is unlikely to have problems of this kind if he or she is able to climb a normal flight of 12 stairs or to walk 50 metres without breathlessness. Even on sightseeing trips elderly people may travel to high altitudes, for example in South America or Nepal where, again, cardiac problems may be exacerbated or unmasked. They may be flown to altitudes of over 3,000 metres (10,000 feet) without time to acclimatise, and this may cause severe and dangerous exacerbations of angina or dyspnoea, as well as acute mountain sickness and life-threatening pulmonary or cerebral oedema.

Peripheral circulation

During prolonged journeys, particularly by air, the elderly person may be immobile for long periods and is therefore more prone to venous thrombosis in the lower limbs. Dehydration due to low humidity in the aircraft cabin, and possibly increased by alcohol consumption during the flight, adds to this likelihood. Long-haul elderly passengers should drink plenty of fluids, avoid alcohol, take frequent walks down the gangways and exercise the legs and feet repeatedly. Oedema of the ankles during long flights is not unknown in younger people, and dependent oedema in older people may be exacerbated.

Renal function

The elderly tend to have diminished renal function which may not be clinically significant under normal circumstances. During travel or in hot climates, dehydration may push them into renal failure and attention to fluid intake is therefore important.

Gastrointestinal problems

The elderly have a reduction in the capacity of their immune system to combat infections including those of the gastrointestinal tract. Some elderly people have reduced gastric acid secretion or take anti-secretory drugs such as H_2 antagonists, for example cimetidine and ranitidine, or proton pump inhibitors, such as omeprazole and lansoprazole, thus adding to their susceptibility to infection. They need to take precautions against food- and waterborne infections, and should be treated with rehydration when these occur.

Locomotor problems

Musculoskeletal problems caused either by osteoarthritis or other conditions may be exacerbated by the physical stress of rushing about in airports or sightseeing. Wheelchairs or electric buggies are available in many airports, provided that such needs are brought to the notice of the airline when booking a flight. They make life much more tolerable for elderly passengers with reduced mobility for musculoskeletal, cardiac or whatever reasons, and some types of aircraft have on-board wheelchairs. Do not expect to find such facilities in every airport. On one occasion, I had to wait with an ill tourist at Kathmandu airport while the only wheelchair available was being used to transport a climber with frostbitten feet — and electric buggies have certainly not yet reached Kathmandu! Prolonged immobility during travel may make arthritic joints very stiff, and every opportunity must be taken to get off the bus to stretch the legs, or to move about in the train or aircraft.

Pre-existing medical problems

Many elderly people take regular medication, often for a variety of conditions. They must ensure that sufficient medication is carried for the length of their journey, possibly with spare supplies in case of loss or theft. Sufficient additional supplies of relief medications, such as nitrates or bronchodilators, should be carried to allow for exacerbations of the condition. Medication must not be carried in check-in baggage that could end its journey on a different continent from the traveller. Rather, it should be carried both about the person and in hand baggage, preferably in more than one location, for example in hand baggage, in a 'bum bag' and in pockets, again in order to avoid total loss or theft. Before departure, instruction should be given about how to deal with crises brought about by the traveller's medical condition while abroad, and a pre-travel health check is most desirable, with a review of medication. Those with disabilities or serious medical conditions should complete a MEDIF form (available from the airline) giving details of their disabilities, otherwise they may be refused a place on the flight on their arrival at the airport.

Insurance

All travellers (see *page 46*), but especially the elderly, should have adequate insurance to cover both emergency treatment abroad and repatriation back to the UK. Elderly travellers should ensure that, as far as possible, any pre-existing medical problems are covered by their policy. This may be difficult to achieve for some conditions, and shopping around and not simply accepting the standard policies offered by tour operators or travel agents may be necessary. Specific support groups, for example the British Diabetic Association, may be able to help. The elderly may need help in reading and interpreting the small print in the insurance they are offered.

Diabetic travellers

Diabetic travellers face many potential problems. They may have difficulty in finding appropriate food. An increase in physical activity on a holiday or on a business trip may lead to hypoglycaemia, while a relaxing holiday with increased food intake may have the opposite effect, leading to loss of diabetic control. Food intake and insulin, or oral medication, may need to be adjusted to take account of these differences. Blood testing and sometimes medication itself may be overlooked in the rush and excitement of travel, and the importance of continuing the usual regime needs to be stressed.

Diabetics are more prone than other travellers to infections, including those of the gastrointestinal tract, and they need to observe scrupulously all the standard precautions regarding food and water hygiene (see *Chapter 1*). In order to avoid infection, even superficial injuries must be carefully tended. Once present, infections may lead to loss of diabetic control. Diabetic travellers must be warned to monitor their control particularly carefully if they become ill.

Crossing time zones

On journeys during which they cross time zones, diabetic travellers must accustom themselves to a longer day if travelling westwards, or a shorter day if travelling eastwards. They must then adjust their physiological diurnal rhythms, and their diet and drug regimes to a new setting on arrival so that they fit in with local time.

Jet lag is the term applied to the difficulty often encountered in adjusting sleep and diurnal rhythms to a new time-scale, and is usually overcome by adjusting eating habits, sleeping times, and so on, to local time as quickly as possible. Diabetics on insulin also need to adjust the times of taking insulin to this new schedule. Different methods of adjustment include the following.

1   Those who take frequent doses of short-acting insulins and adjust dosage by blood sugar testing before each dose may continue to do so during a long journey, taking their longer-acting insulin prior to whatever time they take their sleep period. Diabetics on less frequent doses could also be taught to follow a similar regime.

2   If the day is lengthening during travel, the intervals between

insulin doses could be increased by an appropriate length of time, with the timing of meals also gradually being readjusted until, on arrival, the traveller is in step with local time. At the same time a small increase in each dose would be needed. Conversely, if the day is shortening during travel, insulin doses would need to be reduced a little and the intervals between them reduced also. Similar principles would apply to lengthening or shortening the intervals between doses of oral hypoglycaemic drugs.

3   The diabetic traveller could attempt to adhere to the usual timing of food and insulin dosage or oral drugs during travel, and change to local timing on arrival. This may be difficult to achieve during travel because of the availablity of food at the right times, and an abrupt transition on arrival may cause problems of dosage and possible hypoglycaemia or temporary loss of control.

Changes in the dosage of insulin when crossing time zones may be calculated by one of the following methods:

- a two to four per cent increase or decrease in dose per hour of time change (Sane *et al*, 1990)
- increasing or decreasing intervals by two to three hours for each day of travel (Watkins, 1992)
- adjusting dosage according to blood sugar level before each meal (White, 1994).

Adequate supplies of insulin, syringes or other medication must be carried, with extra allowance for loss. Insulin must not be carried in check-in baggage as it may either be lost or adversely affected by the low temperatures in the baggage hold during flight. All medication and equipment must be carried about the person and/or in hand baggage to ensure its safety. It is often helpful to have an official-looking document worded to the effect that the traveller is carrying syringes, needles, and so on as a matter of medical necessity, in order to satisfy suspicious customs or immigration officials. To cover the possibility of hypoglycaemic attacks it is wise for diabetic travellers to carry a glucagon injection with instructions for its use and/or to have a companion who knows how to handle possible emergencies. A Medic Alert or similar bracelet is strongly advised.

Asthmatic travellers

Depending upon their mode of travel, asthmatics face potential problems as a result of enforced proximity to allergens or irritants ranging from traffic fumes to animals. Whilst on holiday they may also increase the amount of exercise they normally take, or go to environments in which they breathe cold air, both of which may increase asthma symptoms. Like diabetics, they may need to adjust their medication to a new time schedule, or may overlook it in the stress or excitement of travel. They, too, must carry their medication with them and take sufficient additional supplies to cover possible loss or malfunctioning of inhalers. In addition to the usual inhalers, a peak flow meter, a large volume spacer for multi-dose emergency bronchodilator treatment, an emergency supply of steroid tablets and a written self-management plan will enable the asthmatic to travel confidently and to deal with most eventualities. The whole kit will fit easily inside the spacer in hand baggage.

There are no contra-indications to any vaccines for asthmatic travellers, unless they have one or more of the other general contra-indications.

Epileptic travellers

Once again, similar principles apply. Preventive medication must be continued and fitted into any new time schedules during travel and on arrival. A Medic Alert bracelet and an emergency supply of anticonvulsant drugs, probably in the form of rectal diazepam, are useful additions to the epileptic's equipment for travel.

Again there are no contra-indications to any vaccines solely on account of epilepsy, but some anti-malarial drugs such as chloroquine and mefloquine are contra-indicated.

Female travellers

Some of the problems faced by female travellers, particularly when travelling alone, may be more social or cultural than medical, but female travellers should be prepared for them. In some countries it is not usual for women to travel unaccompanied by men and to do so may attract undue attention or make them 'fair game' for unwanted attention from men. Codes of dress are easily transgressed by women in western-style clothing, particularly in hot countries. To bare too much arm or leg may give religious or social offence, or invite sexual overtures.

Adequate menstrual hygiene may prove more difficult to achieve during travel, and suitable supplies of tampons or towels may not always be available. Normal vulvo-vaginal hygiene standards may not be achieved and infections such as thrush may arise.

Oral contraceptives, if taken, should be carried to cover the whole journey as familiar brands, or any at all, may not always be available. In view of the widespread distribution of HIV infection and other sexually-transmitted diseases, casual sex with fellow travellers or local people is to be avoided but if it occurs, using a condom will offer some protection. If a woman becomes dehydrated through heat, or travels to high altitude, it is possibile that the thrombogenic effect of oral contraceptives may be increased. Reduced urine output in hot climates may also predispose to urinary tract infection.

Pregnancy

The middle trimester of pregnancy is probably the most suitable period for foreign travel. At this time most of the risk of miscarriage is past and later complications have not begun to occur. Travel will not increase the risk of early miscarriage, but travelling without proper management of the condition during early pregnancy may give rise to inconvenience at best and danger to life at worst. After 28 weeks of pregnancy a woman will need a medical certificate in order to fly, and after 34 to 35 weeks most international airlines will not carry her.

Factors such as prolonged immobility during long-distance travel and dehydration during flights or in hot climates, increase the likelihood of venous thrombosis in the pregnant woman. Attempts should be made to reduce the effects of immobility and dehydration by drinking copious fluids and frequently moving about. Once again, reduced urine output may lead to urinary tract infection.

Live vaccines should not normally be given to pregnant women, though in situations of very high risk polio or yellow fever vaccines may be given as the risk to the foetus may be higher from the disease than from the vaccine (consult *BNF*, Mehta, 1998; or the 'Green Book', DoH, 1996a, if in doubt). In such situations, careful consideration should be given as to whether travel is really necessary. It is important that, if indicated, anti-malarial drugs are taken, as malaria may be more severe during pregnancy and carries a high risk to the foetus. Chloroquine and proguanil may be given at any stage of pregnancy and mefloquine may be used during the second and third trimesters. Rigorous anti-mosquito precautions are also essential for the pregnant woman. Once again, consideration should be given as to whether travel during pregnancy to an area where malaria is highly endemic is strictly necessary.

Disabled travellers

Many people with disabilities will be able to travel freely with a little forethought and planning. Travel agents, tour operators, bus and train operators and airlines will need to be consulted about provision for those with specific types of disability, and any special needs such as wheelchair facilities at airports or on board aircraft should be booked in advance.

Blindness and deafness

These conditions carry their own obvious problems for the traveller. For deaf people, the inability to understand auditory or visual instructions and messages and, for blind people, difficulty in finding their way around an unfamiliar station, airport or aircraft, or using unfamiliar toilet facilities of the type found in aircraft are obvious examples. An experienced companion is invaluable for all but the most seasoned and determined.

Physical disabilities

The secret of success for the physically disabled traveller is to ensure well ahead that each stage of the journey, however small, is planned in advance and that all the necessary facilities are available. For example, all new or refurbished railway stations in the UK are obliged to provide access for disabled passengers to and from the station, but on unmanned stations access ramps for wheelchairs to and from the train are not available.

With a few exceptions, those travelling outside Northern Europe, North America, Scandinavia, Australia and New Zealand, will probably not find — and should not at present expect — that their disabilities will be catered for as they are in their home countries. Facilities may be poor and many, such as disabled toilets and wheelchair ramps or lifts, will probably not be available at all. This will be true of much of Asia and Africa, with the possible exception of South Africa.

Insurance

All travellers must make sure that they are adequately covered by insurance for medical expenses including, if necessary, repatriation to the UK for treatment. Cover for pre-existing conditions may sometimes be difficult to obtain, but bodies such as the British Diabetic Association are often able to recommend sympathetic insurers. If insurance cover is offered by a tour operator it is necessary to read all the small print carefully, to understand exactly what cover is being offered. Travellers must not assume that all their needs are covered without reading the conditions attached to the insurance, or asking to see the master policy. They must be advised to ask for help in finding out exactly what cover is on offer if they have difficulty in reading, seeing or understanding the policy documents. Medical care may be extremely expensive. Even in countries with which the UK has a reciprocal arrangement for healthcare, and where the UK citizen is entitled to whatever care the citizens of the host country have available to them, travellers must not assume that healthcare will be free of charge.

Purpose of travel

Package holidays

Many of those who take package holidays give little thought to the possible health risks involved, apart from having the few injections recommended by their travel agent or tour operator whose advice is usually inadequate or out of date. More often than not, they travel to destinations with a hot climate and frequently indulge in the avid pursuit of the 'four s's': sun, sea, sand and sex, all of which carry their own risks. In addition, cheap or new varieties of alcohol carry their own temptations and add to the likelihood of risks from the other activities. Many of these risks are covered more fully in other chapters.

Overexposure to UV radiation in sunlight not only causes burning which can ruin a holiday, but also predisposes to skin cancer in the long term. The sea can provide a hazard — water contaminated with raw sewage may be swallowed, and the bites or stings of sea creatures may cause illness. Seafood, especially shellfish such as oysters and mussels, may cause gastrointestinal infections. In some areas, including the Caribbean, contact between skin and sand contaminated with animal faeces may give rise to cutaneous larva migrans, in which worm larvae that do not normally use the human as a host, penetrate the skin and move around looking for somewhere to go, causing intense irritation and a visible track.

The hazards of casual sexual contact while abroad, whether with fellow travellers or with local people, cannot be emphasised too strongly. There is a host of sexually-transmitted diseases waiting to be acquired in addition to the more widely-known risks of HIV and hepatitis B. The effects of alcohol make it all the more likely that a holidaymaker will indulge in behaviour which will predispose to other risks such as casual sex, falling asleep in the sun, or accidents.

Hiring cars, motor cycles or scooters presents a considerable risk in many of the popular holiday destinations due to poor vehicle maintenance, lack of crash helmets, the poor condition of roads and a lack of — or disregard for — traffic regulations. In some countries, the tourist is assumed to be in the wrong whatever the circumstances of an accident. Even if the tourist avoids motorised transport, riding a bicycle (often available for hire), or simply crossing a road as a pedestrian may result in an accident. Traffic on the 'wrong' side of the road in most countries, and the attitude of drivers of motor vehicles who do not observe traffic signals, the rules of the road, or even marked pedestrian crossings, all contribute to the considerable risk of involvement in an accident for the unwary cyclist or pedestrian.

Ineffective or badly-maintained cookers or heaters may be further sources of accidents, and it is not at all unknown for tourists to fall from hotel balconies, either while under the influence of alcohol or simply as the result of leaning on an insubstantial balustrade. Swimming accidents are more likely following alcohol consumption, and serious spinal injuries occur from time to time when holidaymakers dive into too shallow a pool or into sea where there are rocks hidden below the surface.

While a number of those taking package holidays may be experienced travellers, many are not. Inexperienced travellers may need to be reminded of the risks associated with their holiday and advised on how best to avoid or deal with them.

Activity holidays

A glance at the holiday pages of the Sunday newspapers will show that there is now a multitude of companies offering special activity holidays. Vacations incorporating such varied activities as walking, trekking, climbing, caving, cycling, canoeing, sailing, windsurfing, diving, parascending, hang gliding, winter sports, and a variety of other physical or intellectual pursuits all figure regularly in their columns. Many of the participants will be experienced and will know more of the potential hazards of their chosen activity than does their GP or practice nurse, but some may need advice. Those travelling to mountain environments may need advice about high altitude or cold conditions, and those indulging in water sports may need advice on how to deal with drowning, or near drowning and immersion hypothermia. Many activities are potentially dangerous and advice on first aid treatment of trauma may be needed. Many will travel to hot climates for their chosen activity and will need advice about the problems which this may pose, indeed sun may be a hazard for many of them whether in a hot or a cold environment. These risks are addressed in *Chapter 2*.

The travel adviser should ensure that adequate insurance has been taken out in order to cover any possible illness or injury due to the chosen activity, including repatriation if necessary. In other countries, rescue services (if they exist at all) are not necessarily free of charge as they are in the UK, and medical treatment may prove to be very expensive.

Working abroad

The requirements of those intending to work abroad will vary enormously. Not only may they travel to a wide variety of different destinations, but also both their length of stay and their living and working conditions may be equally variable.

Short business trips

The short-term business traveller may be sent abroad at short notice and may visit more than one country during a trip. This makes it difficult to offer preventive advice and vaccination, or adequate malaria prophylaxis, given that vaccines take about two weeks to reach protective antibody levels, and anti-malarial drugs need to be started at least a week before travelling, and preferably longer if mefloquine is being taken for the first time.

It may be possible to educate companies or their employees to give more notice of their intentions. Where this is not feasible, it might be possible to make arrangements with companies for their frequent travellers to be kept up to date with all the vaccinations they are most likely to need, and for the appropriate anti-malarial drugs to be readily available to them. Business travellers are also likely to be entertained during their stay, with all the attendant risks from food and over-indulgence in alcohol. Though it may not be appropriate for longer trips, if they are travelling for a short time, for an extremely important business meeting that would be wrecked if they were ill, the possibility of prophylactic antibacterial therapy for travellers' diarrhoea may need to be considered, using (preferably) ciprofloxacin, or co-trimoxazole. Jet lag due to changing time zones may be a problem for this type of traveller and it may be advisable, if at all possible, to allow two or three days after travelling in which to acclimatise to local time before any important business is done.

Travelling or working abroad in the medium term

Travellers in this category are often young and engaged in prolonged backpacking trips, voluntary or paid aid work. They may be abroad for periods of up to a year and tend to pass through recognisable stages in their adjustment to their new environment.

Those, such as aid workers, who are staying in one place, may initially be overcome with excitement at all the new sights and sensations around them. However, such emotions are all too often replaced by a stage in which fear of illness or for personal safety, frustration when things do not happen in the same way as they do at home, loneliness and homesickness take over. It is important that, before travelling abroad, these travellers should be prepared by counselling for this stage, and that they should be able to maintain contact through this difficult period with their organisation, with other expatriates and with those at home. Eventually such feelings begin to subside and then a state of precarious truce with one's surroundings is reached, to be followed later by an acceptance of the country and its customs, and adjustment to them. This may all take some months to achieve and, for some, a period of only a year may not be long enough for full adjustment to take place. It is this process of reaction and adjustment that is sometimes referred to as culture shock.

Those who are taking a prolonged backpacking trip may face other problems. Released from the constraints of family, country and familiar social patterns of behaviour, they may indulge in risk-taking behaviour in terms of lack of regard for health precautions and potentially dangerous indulgence in sex, drugs and alcohol. They may make and break new relationships as they travel around, and this may add to their problems.

Working abroad in the long term

The problems of those who live for a longer period in a foreign environment are somewhat different. In general, they will have adequate time to arrange for their healthcare before leaving, but they may also take their families along and preventive care will need to be targetted at them as well. As a result, the dilemmas involved in vaccination and anti-malarial treatment for children and possibly for pregnant women (— or for those who may subsequently become pregnant), are introduced. Decisions may have to be made about the suitability of the proposed housing and environment for young children or for a pregnancy and birth, and about whether the family should travel together or be separated for a prolonged period. Advice and counselling are not always forthcoming from employers and the family may turn to medical advisers for help.

As for medium-term travellers, culture shock may be a problem, but with the longer period of stay there is more likelihood of adjustment taking place. However, during the period of adjustment the individual has to continue to work in the new environment and this may be the cause of a great deal of frustration, anger and a sense of helplessness in the face of apparently overwhelming odds. Once again, the support of the employer or organisation and of other expatriates is vital. It is also important that realistic and limited goals are set in the area of work so that no individual feels that he or she is trying to alter the whole social or business fabric of the country single-handed.

When a spouse accompanies the expatriate worker, great stress may be placed on the relationship. It is therefore most important that individuals intending to travel and work together abroad as couples are both psychologically suited to the task, and that their relationship is strong enough to survive the experience. Pre-travel counselling is extremely important for both partners. A spouse who has to give up employment or leave a familiar circle of friends or relatives in order to travel, may feel the loss of role acutely, or react psychologically as though bereaved by the loss of relationships.

Those who have undergone previous psychiatric illness, such as depression or psychotic illnesses, and those with a history of severe stress reactions, personality disorders or alcohol problems, may break down under the stress of cultural readjustment and it would be wise for them not to be posted abroad.

Children often adjust to a new environment remarkably well, but at first are likely to need the stability of established relationships with well-known people — especially the continued presence of at least one parent or familiar adult, and well-loved objects such as favourite toys. Adolescents are more likely to be disturbed by major changes of environment and it may be better not to inflict such changes on them, even if it involves splitting the family and a resultant stay with relatives or at a boarding school in the home country.

Before either taking the decision to relocate a family abroad, or contemplating the possibility of starting a family abroad, it is important to consider the potential health risks existing in the chosen country as well as the vaccinations likely to be needed and the choice of anti-malarials. The specific needs of small children and pregnant women must be taken into account in each of these areas of risk. The chapters about sources of infection, vaccination and malaria address these problems in greater detail.

Returning home

Returning home is not necessarily a problem for prolonged back-packers. They may not have stayed for long periods in any one place and they often have a good reason for a planned return home, such as a place in higher education or a job. However, for the longer-stay traveller who has passed through the process of adjustment, it may be equally difficult to readjust to returning home. This type of traveller will probably have changed as a result of his or her experiences, and circumstances as well as people left behind at home may well have altered from their pre-travel state. Debriefing and a period of readjustment are important, and it is essential to realise that it is not simply a matter of taking up situations and relationships where they were left off.

Those in pursuit of recreational drugs

For those individuals who may be travelling with the pursuit of recreational drugs in mind, it is wise to counsel them not only about the risks involved in the drugs themselves and in the sharing of needles by injecting drug users, but also about the risks either of being caught in possession of drugs, or of trying to take drugs across borders. The penalties may vary from long terms of imprisonment in squalid surroundings, to death. Young travellers, and indeed all travellers, should be warned that in no circumstances should they carry even the most innocent-looking package across any border for another person.

Sex tourism

Many travellers set off abroad with the express intention of having sexual adventures with the same or the opposite sex. Several South-East Asian countries, such as Thailand, are among their favourite destinations. The obvious risks of contracting sexually-transmitted diseases from such behaviour are enormous. There is also a group of travellers who could be called 'inadvertent sex tourists'. These are those who fall prey to sexual temptation, or have sexual entertainment presented to them by their hosts without having anticipated it. Among those tourists who plan sex, behaviour may vary from repeated contacts with a variety of different partners to a virtually monogamous relationship with one person throughout the stay. Some travellers go abroad to enjoy the kinds of pleasure denied them at home, for example sex with under-age boys or girls. They may be denied a sexual outlet in their home environment, but feel more free to indulge in whatever is their orientation while abroad.

There is a high — and increasing — prevalence of HIV and other sexually-transmissible infections in the sex workers of Asia, Africa and wherever else sex tourism takes place, and the risks are obvious. In spite of this there is a very low rate of condom usage by travellers of both sexes, and this appears to be irrespective of their knowledge of the dangers and of their normal patterns of behaviour at home.

Activities involving children may be reduced as legislation in some countries aims to prosecute those who, whilst abroad, commit what would be regarded as sexual offences at home. Much remains to be done by travel clinic staff and others to warn potential planned or inadvertent sex tourists of the risks which they run, and to encourage safer sexual practices including the use of condoms.

Sexually-transmitted diseases (STDs)

The term 'sexually-transmitted disease' is used to refer to a disease spread chiefly by sexual contact. Many different organisms may be transmitted in this way — from viruses to parasites, and there is a wide range of diseases which they may cause.

STDs and travel

Travel has long been associated with the spread of infectious diseases in general and STDs in particular. Migrants, invading armies, sailors and, in more modern times, truck drivers are all implicated by the spread of STDs. Now that world travel is open to more and more tourists and business travellers, they too play their part. The rapidity of air travel now enables travellers to bring their acquired diseases back home more rapidly and to distribute them to their spouses and other contacts, perhaps even before being aware of their existence themselves.

HIV infection

The syndrome that became known as AIDS (Acquired Immune Deficiency Syndrome) was first described in 1981, but there is evidence that occasional cases existed some years before that date (WHO, 1996). By the end of 1995, it was estimated that some 6 million cases of AIDS had already occurred, and that some 17 million individuals had been infected with HIV worldwide. It is thought that the disease may have originated in Africa, from whence it may have travelled to Haiti and thence to the USA and elsewhere. There may also have been direct spread from Africa to Europe.

Current patterns of spread have been described as follows (Mann, 1988).

Type I Spread occurs in western Europe, North America, Australia and New Zealand. Homosexual and bisexual men are chiefly involved in sexual transmission, though heterosexual spread also occurs and is increasing. Since donated blood is now screened, the main blood-borne means of spread is through the sharing of needles by injecting drug users.

Type II Spread occurs in Africa, South America and the Caribbean. Here the main sources of infection are heterosexual contact, mother-to-child transmission and infected blood transfusions.

Type III Spread occurs in Asia, North Africa, the Middle East and Eastern Europe. Here, the principal sources of spread are imported ones: from imported blood and from those coming from other infected areas. But spread by prostitutes and injecting drug-users is increasing in these areas.

Although any of the groups of travellers mentioned above may be responsible for spreading HIV infection, the concept of 'core groups' that can infect large numbers of other individuals, is important. These core groups include sailors, long-distance truck drivers, migrants, prostitutes, and the sexual partners of these groups.

HIV and other STDs

The traveller who is exposed to HIV infection will probably have been exposed at the same time to the risk of other STDs. Different STDs may interact with HIV in a number of ways. First of all, the likelihood of transmission of HIV is increased by the presence of other STDs. This may be the result of damage either to mucus membranes in the genital tract allowing access to HIV, or to influences on the immune system. Secondly, the course of HIV infection may be altered by the presence of other STDs so that it progresses more rapidly. Finally, the course of other STDs may be altered by the suppression of the immune system caused by HIV infection.

Non-sexual spread of HIV

Travellers may be more prone to HIV infection in countries where the infection is highly prevalent and blood for transfusion is not adequately screened. Plasma and other blood products carry a similar risk of HIV infection. Synthetic plasma expanders (such as Haemaccel) do not carry the same risk and may be used, for example, while awaiting repatriation to the home country for treatment. Other ways of avoiding the risk may be the storage and use of one's own blood or the use of 'clean' donors from a pool of known donors. These methods are more appropriate to long-term expatriates than to most other travellers. The Blood Care Foundation (see *page 162*) undertakes to deliver 'clean' blood to its members, but its cover is not yet worldwide. The re-use of disposable syringes and needles and the improper sterilisation of re-usable injection and other medical/ surgical equipment carry a risk of transmitting HIV infection. The risks to injecting drug users of sharing needles are well known in the UK and are just as great, if not greater, elsewhere. It may be advisable for travellers going to areas with high endemicity of HIV, to areas where blood is not adequately screened, or to areas where standards of sterilisation and use of equipment are not high, to carry a sterile kit containing syringes, needles, an intravenous cannula and a drip set. Skin sutures and/or adhesive closures and sterile dressings may also be added. Such sets are available commercially or may be prepared in the travel clinic for sale to travellers.

Sexual transmission of HIV

In Type I countries (see *page 54*), HIV infection is often considered to be a problem mainly affecting the homosexual community. This, of course, is not entirely true in those countries and it is certainly not true in other countries, where sex between men and women is a major route of transmission of the infection. Genital or orogenital contact with local people of either sex, particularly in Africa and increasingly in South-East Asia and elsewhere, is to be avoided. Sex with fellow travellers is also a potential source of infection as they may have been exposed to infection before or during their journey. Prostitutes have a particularly high prevalence rate of HIV infection. The sex industry comes in many guises, and bar girls and hostesses are often prostitutes by another name. Condoms offer some degree of protection and should be carried and their use insisted upon by both males and females at risk. Their use is often neglected, whether sex is the main objective of the traveller or whether it occurs spontaneously and unexpectedly. The use of alcohol is often associated with sexual adventures which would not otherwise have been embarked upon.

Other viral STDs

Hepatitis B

Hepatitis B may be transmitted by all the same routes as HIV, and is much more easily transmissible. However, unlike HIV, vaccination is available. Vaccination should be offered both to all those whose lifestyle make it likely that they will be exposed to infection while travelling, and to those long-stay expatriates whose length of stay or conditions of living will expose them to a greater possibility of trauma, to inadequate medical facilities, or to a search for the companionship of sexual partners.

Human papilloma virus (HPV)

HPV is a very widespread sexually-transmitted virus and infection with it is probably the commonest of all STD infections worldwide. Genital warts are the clinical manifestation of infection, but many infections are subclinical and individuals may be infectious to others without their knowledge. The danger of HPV infection lies in the fact that it predisposes females to carcinoma of the cervix.

Herpes virus

This, again, is a common sexually-transmitted virus. One strain is predominantly sexually transmitted, and another may be acquired by non-sexual transmission, but the latter may also be sexually transmitted, for example by orogenital contact. Transmission from mother to baby may have serious consequences in the neonatal period.

Bacterial STDs

Chlamydia

The most common type of STD in both the UK and the USA is non-gonococcal urethritis in the male, and cervicitis in the female caused by Chlamydia. In the female it may go on to produce pelvic inflammatory disease. If diagnosed it is relatively easily treated with tetracyclines or erythromycin-type antibiotics. It probably occurs frequently elsewhere in the world, but its prevalence is not fully known.

In Africa, India, South-East Asia, South America, the Caribbean, and occasionally elsewhere, Chlamydia causes lymphogranuloma venereum in which a small genital lesion, which may not always be apparent, leads to the formation of large swellings in the inguinal lymph nodes. This may be followed by ulceration and further complications.

Gonorrhoea

Gonococcal infection has generally declined in frequency in the last thirty or forty years, but is still a problem in developed countries as strains resistant to penicillin and even to newer drugs, such as ciprofloxacin, emerge. It is still a common sexually-transmitted infection in developing countries. While usually symptomatic in the male, with urethritis and discharge, it is often symptomless in the female. Non-genital infection, such as tonsillitis, and complications elsewhere in the body, such as gonococcal arthritis, may occur, and mother-to-baby transmission during birth may result in infection of the eyes (ophthalmia neonatorum).

Syphilis

Syphilis has also been in decline but, in recent years, a recrudescence has occurred, principally in the USA. The disease is still prevalent in developing countries. The causative organism, Treponema pallidum, is sensitive to penicillin. The primary lesion on the genitalia or elsewhere is a painless sore or chancre which may be followed within a few weeks by a maculopapular rash. The later stages of syphilis can affect virtually any bodily system or organ, with potentially destructive results.

Chancroid

Chancroid occurs more commonly worldwide than does syphilis. In it a painful, small lesion — usually on the genitalia — progresses to ulceration, possibly with enlargement of the inguinal lymph nodes. The causative organism, Haemophilus ducreyi, is sensitive to erythromycin and some cephalosporin antibiotics.

Granuloma inguinale (Donovanosis)

In granuloma inguinale, the initial skin nodule progresses locally to granulating ulceration, sometimes with remote blood-borne spread. It is largely a problem in developing countries and is sensitive to a variety of antibiotics.

Other sexually-transmitted infections

Many other organisms that are not usually considered as causes of sexually-transmitted diseases may be transmissible in this way. Candida and Trichomonas are obvious examples but many other infections, such as hepatitis A and infections of the gut including dysentery, amoebiasis and giardiasis, may be acquired sexually. Pubic lice and scabies may also be acquired.

UK immigrants returning to their country of origin

Immigrants going back to their home countries are at particular risk of becoming ill when returning home to visit their families. If they are returning to malarial areas they often omit to take any precautions against mosquito bites, or to take anti-malarial drugs. Their relatives, who are probably at least partially immune to malaria as a result of prolonged exposure, do not use such precautions, but the returning immigrants themselves lose their immunity within a few months of leaving the malarial area. They may also be at risk from potentially vaccine-preventable and other diseases, but may not see any reason for protecting themselves for what they perceive as a return to the familiar environment of their home country or to the safety of the home of their parents or grandparents. It may be difficult in areas with a large immigrant population to persuade returning immigrants to consult a doctor or nurse. Information leaflets and posters written using appropriate languages and displayed on the practice premises, may help to spread information. The co-operation of religious or other community leaders, and articles or advertising (written using the relevant languages) in local newspapers or periodicals, may also be helpful.

4

Travel vaccinations

Vaccination and immunity

The first consideration to enter the minds of many potential travellers is, 'What jabs will I need?' Vaccinations will protect travellers against only about five per cent of the health risks awaiting them outside our shores, but knowledge of the basic principles underlying immunity and vaccination is essential for an understanding of this important aspect of travel health.

Pathogenic organisms invading the body carry antigens that provoke the host into producing antibodies against them. These antibodies, produced by B cell lymphocytes, attach themselves chemically to the antigen, each type of antibody fitting a specific antigen like a key fitting a lock. Antibodies attached to antigens on the invading organism attack the organism directly and also make it more susceptible to attack by cytotoxic cells that attack it and phagocytic cells that 'eat' it. T cell lymphocytes are also mobilised and act in two ways. One type directly attacks cells infected by virus particles, and the other type mobilises more B cells to produce antibodies (see *Figure 4.1*).

Figure 4.1: The immune system's response to an invading organism

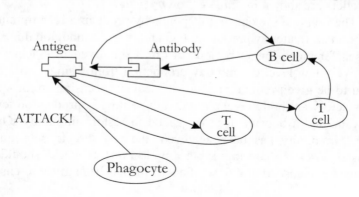

Immunity is produced either by exposure to a disease itself, with subsequent persistence of antibodies, or by a process of immunisation in which exposure to the disease is imitated in some way. Immunisation may be active, in which case a live but modified organism, a killed organism or an antigenic portion of an organism is introduced into the body by the process of vaccination. Passive immunisation takes place when antibodies from another source are injected into the individual.

Active immunisation

This produces longer lasting immunity because the individual's immune system is programmed by the process to continue to produce antibodies. It is achieved by the injection or, in some instances, by the oral ingestion of a vaccine that is prepared in one of the following ways:

- from live organisms which have been modified or attenuated so that they remain antigenic but are no longer pathogenic (live vaccines)
- from killed organisms which remain antigenic (inactivated vaccines) or from bacterial toxins which have been chemically inactivated (toxoids)
- from chemical components of organisms rather than the whole organism, such as surface antigens or viral sub-units (single component vaccines).

Examples of these types of vaccine, used for the protection of travellers are shown in *Table 4.1* on *page 63*.

The immune system first responds by producing IgM immunoglobulins and later by producing IgG and IgA immunoglobulins that persist for much longer periods of time. Some vaccines achieve a relatively low level of antibody production from a single dose and need to be given on one or more subsequent occasions to produce satisfactory antibody levels. Eventually, antibody production tends to wane and a booster dose is needed to restore immunity. Once initial immunity has been achieved, the response to subsequent booster doses is more rapid, but a period of two weeks should be allowed to elapse after a dose of a vaccine has been given to ensure

Table 4.1: Travel vaccines	
Live vaccines	

Viral: oral polio
    yellow fever
	Bacterial: BCG
	    oral typhoid

Inactivated vaccines	

Viral: hepatitis A
    rabies
    Japanese B encephalitis
    tick-borne encephalitis
    polio (inactivated)
	Bacterial: typhoid (whole cell)
	    cholera
	    (neither is currently
	    used in the UK)

Inactivated toxins or toxoids	
Viral: none	Bacterial: tetanus diphtheria
Single component vaccines (prepared from a component of the organism)	

Viral (sub-unit): hepatitis B	Bacterial (surface antigen):
	    typhoid (Vi antigen)
	    meningococcal A+C

adequate antibody levels are reached. A further primary course of vaccination is never needed, even if the usual interval for a booster dose has been greatly exceeded.

Passive immunisation

Passive immunisation involves giving antibodies produced by one individual to another individual. This is done by using human normal immunoglobulin (HNIG), a product derived from pooled human blood. The main constituent is IgG. Following an intramuscular dose of HNIG, effective antibody levels are reached in about 24 hours. Because the recipient's immune system has not been programmed to produce further supplies of antibody, protection is relatively short-lived, lasting from four to six months depending on the dosage used.

Indications for travel vaccinations

UK vaccines that should be brought up to date for travel

Tetanus

Tetanus spores are found worldwide in soil, and protection is needed for all destinations. A primary course consists of three doses of 0.5 ml absorbed tetanus toxoid given intramuscularly at intervals of four weeks. The schedule for children includes boosters pre-school and prior to leaving school, and a booster is needed for adults after an interval of ten years. An adult who has received a total of five doses of vaccine should not need another dose unless a potentially tetanus-prone wound occurs, but travellers to countries where contamination of wounds by animal faeces is more likely to occur are often given a booster dose of vaccine if it has not been given in the last ten years, even if they have already received five doses.

Poliomyelitis

Live oral polio vaccine is used in the UK. A primary course consists of three doses at intervals of four weeks. The schedule for children includes booster doses pre-school and prior to leaving school. A booster is needed after ten years for adults who are travelling to areas where polio is endemic and where standards of water hygiene and sewage disposal are less rigorous than they are in western Europe. It is therefore necessary for a very wide range of countries. Inactivated polio vaccine is available unlicensed on a named patient only basis in the UK for those for whom a live vaccine is contra-indicated. The schedule is the same as for oral vaccine but it is given intra-muscularly.

Diphtheria

Diphtheria toxoid is given as part of the child immunisation schedule combined with tetanus and pertussis, with boosters pre-school and before leaving school. Otherwise a primary course would consist of three doses of 0.5 ml at intervals of four weeks. *For adults and children over the age of ten*, the adult vaccine must be used either alone or combined with tetanus as Td (*not* the same as DT used for children). If the adult vaccine is not available, 0.1 ml of the child vaccine may be given. Adults who have not been immunised or had a booster dose in the last ten years should be given the vaccine if they are travelling to developing countries and will be in close personal contact with local people (for example working in teaching or healthcare), or if they are travelling to areas of the former Soviet Union where outbreaks of diphtheria have recently occurred.

Vaccines needed for areas of poor water hygiene and sanitation

Polio has already been mentioned but, along with hepatitis A, typhoid and cholera, it is spread by the faecal/oral route in conditions where drinking water and sewage are not adequately kept apart and/or attention to hygiene is less than scrupulous. Contamination of food, especially shellfish and salads or vegetables washed with contaminated water, may occur. Cholera is extremely uncommon among travellers from the West, the risk being about one in half a million. The risk of typhoid is about one in 50,000 but the risk of hepatitis A is much greater at about one in 300 to 500 (Steffen and Lobel, 1996). All may be avoided by scrupulous food, water and personal hygiene. Indeed, the current cholera vaccine is relatively ineffective and is no longer recommended by the World Health Organization; it is not currently available in the UK.

Hepatitis A

Hepatitis A protection is recommended for travel to all destinations apart from northern and western Europe, North America, Australia and New Zealand.

For short stays of up to two to six months, passive immunisation with immunoglobulin may suffice. The dose for adults is 250 mg for up to two months' protection and 500 mg for up to five months' protection, given intramuscularly.

For longer stays or frequent travellers, active immunisation with inactivated vaccine is a better option. It is given intramuscularly in a dose of 0.5 or 1.0 ml depending on the brand of vaccine used. A single dose gives protection for a year, and a booster dose after six to twelve months extends protection to ten years.

Typhoid

The areas of risk are similar to those for hepatitis A but the level of risk is lower. The area of highest risk for UK travellers appears to be the Indian subcontinent (India, Pakistan, Nepal, Sri Lanka), Africa and Peru. The killed vaccine, not currently available in the UK, is given in two doses of 0.5 ml intramuscularly at an interval of four to six weeks. Protection lasts for three years after which a single booster dose is needed. The vaccine may produce systemic reactions which can be reduced by giving all but the first dose as 0.1 ml intradermally. The Vi capsular antigen vaccine is less prone to systemic effects and is given in a single dose of 0.5 ml intramuscularly, with a similar duration of protection. The oral vaccine is a live vaccine given as three capsules, each taken separately on alternate days with the stomach empty and with a cool (not a hot) drink. This gives protection for one year, though in the USA four capsules are given on alternate days with protection for five years.

Vaccines needed for diseases spread by mosquitoes and ticks

Precautions against insect bites must still be taken when vaccines have been given. Yellow fever is found in South American and African countries situated on a band on either side of the Equator. It is spread by bites from infected mosquitoes. Japanese B encephalitis is found from the Indian subcontinent and in a broad band eastwards through South-East Asia, though not now in Japan. It is most likely to occur in the wet season in rural areas and is a risk for longer-stay travellers. Measures taken to avoid mosquito bites include covering exposed skin, using insect repellents and sleeping under a mosquito net. Tick-borne encephalitis is transmitted by tick bites and is found chiefly in central and eastern Europe and also in northern Europe and Scandinavia, mainly in forested areas. Tick bites are more likely to occur in warm weather in walkers with unprotected limbs.

Yellow fever

Yellow fever vaccine is a live virus vaccine that can be given only in a registered Yellow Fever Vaccination Centre, though any practice or travel clinic may apply to become a Centre. Affected countries require a certificate of vaccination as a condition of entry, as do some non-affected countries if a traveller is entering from an infected area (these countries may have the species of mosquito which is able to transmit yellow fever should the infection be introduced). The vaccine should be given to all travellers to yellow fever areas even if it is not a condition of entry. The vaccine is given in a dose of 0.5 ml by deep subcutaneous injection and protection lasts for ten years.

Japanese B encephalitis

The risk of acquiring this infection is low for most travellers, but the vaccine should be recommended to those who will be spending long periods (that is of four weeks or more) in the rural areas of affected countries in the wet season when mosquitoes are more numerous. The vaccine is not licensed in the UK and must be obtained on a named patient basis. The dosage is three doses of 1 ml with the second and third doses given seven and twenty-eight to thirty days after the first, though two doses at intervals of one to four weeks give a high measure of protection if time is pressing. Severe allergic or neurological reactions occasionally occur. The risk of acquiring the disease as a traveller is similar to the risk of having a severe reaction to the vaccine.

Tick-borne encephalitis

This vaccine should be recommended to travellers to those countries ranging from Austria and Germany in the west to the western former Soviet Union countries in the east and to Scandinavia in the north if they are likely to be walking in forest areas, particularly in the summer. The dosage is two doses of 0.5 ml at intervals of four to twelve weeks, to give protection for a year. A booster dose after nine to twelve months prolongs protection to three years. The vaccine is not licensed in the UK but is available on a named patient basis.

Vaccines needed for diseases associated with close personal contact

Diphtheria has already been discussed. Meningococcal disease and tuberculosis are also spread by nasopharyngeal droplet infection.

They occur more frequently in developing countries and the risk is greater the longer the stay (particularly if it is greater than four weeks) and the closer the contact with the local population.

Tuberculosis

A detailed account of BCG vaccination is outside the scope of this book as it is unlikely to form part of the work of most GP travel clinics. Most younger people born in the UK will be protected and will bear the scar of BCG vaccination. If this is absent and the individual intends to stay for a prolonged period in Africa, Asia or South America — particularly in close contact with the local population — it would be wise to arrange skin testing and to give BCG vaccine if the result is negative.

Meningococcal disease

The indications for this vaccine are similar to those for BCG and diphtheria. In addition, Muslim pilgrims on the Haj pilgrimage to Mecca require the vaccine together with a certificate of vaccination as a condition of travel. It is wise to offer it to those taking trekking holidays in Nepal as well as to travellers in sub-Saharan Africa, particularly children and young adults who are most at risk of meningococcal infection. A single dose of 0.5 ml given intramuscularly gives protection for three to five years.

Vaccines needed for long-term travellers or expatriates, or for travel to remote areas

Hepatitis B

Hepatitis B is spread by sexual contact, by the sharing of needles by intravenous drug users, by injections or other physically invasive medical or surgical procedures and by infected blood or blood products. The risk is greater outside western Europe, North America, Australia and New Zealand, and for long-term or remote travellers who are more likely to need medical or surgical treatment in questionable surroundings. Body piercing and tattooing are also potential sources of infection. The vaccine is a sub-unit virus vaccine given in three doses of 1.0 ml intramuscularly, with the second and third doses given one and six months after the first dose. This gives protection for ten years, but it is advisable to check antibody levels two months after completing the course, as protective antibody levels are found in only eighty to ninety per cent of those vaccinated. If time is pressing when the traveller first presents, the third dose may be given one month after the second, but a booster would then be needed a year later.

Rabies

Rabies does not present a high level of risk for the traveller but is fatal if it occurs. It is acquired by a bite, a scratch or even, on occasions, a lick from an infected animal — often, though not invariably, from a dog. Monkeys and a variety of small mammals, including vampire bats in South America, may pass on the virus. Apart from parts of Europe (including the UK) and a few parts of Asia and the Americas, the risk of rabies is worldwide, though greatest in Africa and most of Asia and South America. Those working with animals are at highest risk but long-term travellers, those going to remote (especially rural) areas, backpackers and trekkers are also at risk. The vaccine is an inactivated virus vaccine derived from human cell culture and is given in three doses of 1.0 ml intramuscularly, with the second and third doses at intervals of seven and twenty-eight days after the first. Protection lasts for three years. A dose of 0.1 ml may be given intradermally at the same intervals (though this is not a licensed dosage), and an emergency rapid course of 0.1 ml intradermally into each of the four limbs on the same day also gives a high level of protection. Two intramuscular doses at an interval of four weeks give protection for a large majority of individuals and this regime may be used if cost is a major issue. Post-exposure vaccination is needed in the event of a bite from a potentially-infected animal whether pre-exposure vaccination is given or not, but pre-exposure vaccination will reduce the number of post-exposure doses needed and will buy a little time for the traveller to obtain treatment. These factors are important for travellers to remote areas and for those in countries where the only vaccine available is derived from animal tissue and is associated with a much higher rate of adverse reactions than the human diploid cell vaccine.

Adverse reactions to the human vaccine may occur and occasional neurological complications are reported.

Vaccination schedules

When preparing a vaccination schedule, much will depend on the time-scale allowed by the traveller's departure date. Most vaccines will need up to two weeks to produce maximally protective antibody levels, whereas passive immunisation (for example for hepatitis A) gives protection within twenty-four to forty-eight hours and would be more appropriate for a late attender provided that the journey was not to be prolonged beyond the effectiveness of the immunoglobulin.

In the case of vaccines needing more than one dose, or for prolonged journeys during which a booster dose would be needed, it may sometimes be possible to advise the traveller to complete the course during the journey if it is known that the vaccine will be available at the correct stage of the journey. For those travellers who attend late and need hepatitis B or rabies protection, the shortened courses given above may be used. If the price of rabies vaccine is a major issue, the cost may be reduced if several travellers can be vaccinated by the intradermal route at the same clinic, thereby allowing several doses to be taken from a single ampoule.

Live vaccines must be given on the same day, or with an interval of at least three weeks between them; inactivated or single component vaccines may be given on the same day as each other and on the same day as live vaccines. For up to two weeks after the giving of a vaccine there may be a period of somewhat reduced response to another vaccine, so it is better to give vaccines needed at a similar time on the same day rather than spreading the doses over several days. If yellow fever protection is needed, the timing of other vaccinations will need to be fitted in around that, particularly if the patient has to attend a clinic elsewhere for it.

Ideally, travellers who need protection against a wide variety of diseases should present themselves at least eight weeks before departure. This gives time for a full schedule to be planned and given, and also allows adequate antibody levels to develop before departure. The schedule would, of course, be longer if primary courses of polio, tetanus or diphtheria vaccine were needed rather than booster doses. Travel clinic literature and posters should encourage those planning a trip abroad to consult the travel clinic doctor or nurse well in advance of departure.

The vaccines most likely to be recommended for the majority of destinations are tetanus and polio. The most probable 'immunisable' infectious disease for most travellers to acquire is hepatitis A, and protection should be an important part of the schedule for many destinations. Typhoid is a much lower risk for most travellers but will come into many schedules, especially for travellers to the Indian subcontinent, Africa or parts of South America. A full risk assessment for each individual traveller, taking into account the factors of destination, time, duration and mode of travel, the type of accommodation and activities to be undertaken on arrival, will allow the adviser to suggest other vaccinations and precautions that are needed.

Suggested vaccination schedules where adequate time has been allowed (see *Table 4.2* on *page 72*)

The right-hand column refers to individuals who have never received a primary course of polio, tetanus or diphtheria vaccination. If BCG vaccination is needed it should be given on the same day as yellow fever and oral polio vaccines, or at least three weeks before or after them.

Vaccination of children for travel

The minimum ages at which travel vaccines are recommended and the recommended doses are indicated in *Table 4.3* on *page 73*.

Table 4.2: Vaccination schedules

First visit eight weeks before departure (minimum two weeks if only single dose vaccines are needed, or six weeks if hepatitis B or primary courses are not given)

	No primary UK vaccination needed	Primary UK vaccination needed
For all travellers:	oral polio booster tetanus booster	polio (1) tetanus (1)
For some travellers:	diphtheria booster meningococcal A+C (single dose) yellow fever (if a registered centre) hepatitis B (1) rabies (1) Japanese encephalitis (1) tick-borne encephalitis (1)	diphtheria (1)

Second visit one week after the first

	rabies (2) Japanese encephalitis (2)	

Third visit four weeks after the first

	hepatitis B (2) tick-borne encephalitis (2) rabies (3) Japanese encephalitis (3)	polio (2) tetanus (2) diphtheria (2)

Fourth visit eight weeks after the first

	hepatitis B (3)	polio (3) tetanus (3) diphtheria (3)

Table 4.3: Vaccination of children — minimum ages, recommended doses

Vaccine	Minimum age	First dose	Subsequent dose(s) if needed for primary course/ other notes
Typhoid (inactivated) Currently unavailable in UK	1 year	0.25 ml i/m	0.25 ml i/m or 0.1 ml s/c
Typhoid (Vi)	18 months	0.5 ml i/m	
Typhoid (oral)	6 years	1 cap. alt. days x 3	
Hepatitis A (vaccine)	1 year	0.5 ml i/m	Havrix Junior-Avaxim not yet licensed for children
Hepatitis A (HNIG)	No lower limit	125 mg i/m 50 mg i/m or 0.02–0.04 mg/kg	For up to 2 months' trip For up to 5 months' trip Hepatitis A is often mild in young children
Hepatitis B	No lower limit	0.5 ml i/m	Engerix B or HB Vax II
Meningococcal	2 months	0.5 ml i/m	
Japanese encephalitis	No lower limit	0.5 ml s/c	Japanese encephalitis is often severe in children
Tick-borne encephalitis	No lower limit	0.5 ml i/m	
Yellow fever	9 months	0.5 ml	Risk of vaccine encephalitis under 9/12; give only if very great risk
Polio, tetanus and diphtheria: as for UK child immunisation schedule			

Vaccine problems, cautions and contra-indications

Acute febrile illness is a contra-indication to the administration of any vaccine, though minor afebrile illness or, for example, 'snuffles' in children is not. Another absolute contra-indication is a severe reaction to a previous dose of the same vaccine. Such a reaction would be either localised, with redness, swelling and induration affecting most of the circumference of the arm, or generalised, with high fever (39.5 degrees within 48 hours of the dose), collapse, anaphylaxis, bronchospasm, laryngeal oedema or convulsions.

Live vaccines should not be given during pregnancy. If there is a very high risk of polio or yellow fever, the risk may outweigh the possibility of risk to the foetus but an alternative may be not to undertake the journey. Inactivated or component vaccines may be given during pregnancy but there is a small risk that a pyrexial reaction may cause miscarriage.

Live vaccines should not, with few exceptions, be given to those with lowered levels of immunity. Such individuals include:

- those being treated by chemotherapy or radiation for malignant disease, or within six months of such treatment
- those having immunosuppressive treatment following organ transplant
- those who have had bone marrow transplantation in the last six months
- those having taken high dose oral steroid therapy in the last three months (equivalent in children to 2 mg per kg per day for one week, or 1 mg per kg per day for one month. In adults, 40 mg per day for more than one week)
- those with lowered immunity due to blood dyscrasias
- those with immunodeficiency syndromes, for example AIDS.

It would be wise to discuss with the physician in charge of such patients the advisability of vaccination, or of the proposed journey itself.

For HIV positive patients who are not symptomatic, inactivated polio vaccine may be given instead of the live oral vaccine. There is no evidence to support the safety or otherwise of yellow fever vaccine in these individuals; they should not be given BCG vaccination.

Vaccination techniques

Skin cleansing is not usually necessary and if it is used any liquid must evaporate before injection of live vaccines.

The site of choice for intramuscular injections is the deltoid region of the upper arm, though HNIG may be injected deeply into the upper outer quadrant of the buttock in view of its relatively large volume. A 23G needle is appropriate for i/m injection in thin patients and a 25G may be used for small children. A longer 21G needle may be needed if the buttock is used, or for patients with more subcutaneous fat.

In addition, the deltoid region is recommended for intradermal injection, especially for BCG and rabies vaccines, though if the 'emergency' vaccination in all four limbs is used for rabies, the thighs will be used as well. The skin should be stretched taut and the needle inserted with the bevel upwards, just into the thickness of the epidermis almost parallel to the skin surface, for about two millimetres. Care should be taken that the needle is not 'blown' off the syringe as there is a good deal of resistance to injection. If the injection is successful, a raised and blanched bleb will be produced with a diameter of about 7 millimetres for a 0.1 ml injection.

Storage of vaccines

Vaccines must be stored according to manufacturers' instructions, usually at between four and eight degrees Celsius. They should be kept in a lockable pharmacy or vaccine refrigerator with an external maximum/minimum thermometer, and should not be kept in door pockets but on the shelves. Domestic refrigerators are not suitable for vaccine storage. Room should be allowed for circulation of air around the vaccines. The storage temperature must not be allowed to fall to or below freezing point. Freezing will cause considerable damage and loss of potency of vaccines. Short periods at room temperature are much less damaging to vaccines than is freezing, but fluctuations in temperature should be avoided by refraining from unnecessary opening of the refrigerator or from leaving the door open. If the refrigerator is not overcrowded, other drugs may be stored in it but food and drink should not be stored in the same refrigerator as vaccines.

Purchase and stock control of vaccines

A simple audit of vaccine use will provide an estimate of the quantities of vaccines likely to be used and bulk purchases may then be made direct from the manufacturers, usually at a good rate of discount if orders are sufficiently large. For those vaccines which are reimbursable by the Prescription Pricing Authority (PPA) a profit will be made on each dose given, particularly if a good discount has been obtained from the supplier. The cost of vaccines not reimbursed by the PPA should be passed on to the patient and it is reasonable to add a margin of at least ten per cent to the NHS cost price to reflect the same profit margin which is obtained from the PPA for reimbursable vaccines.

A policy must be drawn up in consultation with the practice manager and all staff involved in running the clinic, covering the level of stock of each vaccine which will trigger its re-ordering. Responsibility should be assigned to a member of the team for carrying out the policy and for checking on expiry dates of vaccines in stock. The policy should set out the time intervals at which checks of stocks will be made and the method of documentation to be used for checking and ordering. This type of procedure will be familiar to dispensing practices, but will be new ground for many other practices.

5

Malaria

Malaria is, in terms of both morbidity and mortality, the most important tropical disease spread by insects for both travellers and indigenous peoples. Its causative organism is the protozoal parasite Plasmodium, usually transmitted to humans by bites from the female anopheline mosquito which is the intermediate host for the parasite. There are four species of Plasmodium: P falciparum, P vivax, P ovale and P malariae. Anopheline mosquitoes breed in hot climates where there is standing water in which their larval stage lives. The disease does not occur in temperate climates or at higher altitudes in tropical or subtropical countries, where ambient temperatures are lower.

The parasite is injected into humans by female mosquitoes when they alight on the skin to take a blood meal. Parasites are injected in their thousands in the form of sporozoites from the mosquito's salivary glands. Within a few hours the sporozoites have disappeared from the blood to enter the liver where they divide repeatedly to form schizonts which contain thousands of daughter cells called merozoites. This process is called pre-erythrocytic schizogony. On maturation the schizonts rupture to release merozoites into the blood where they become attached to and enter red blood cells. Within the red cells the merozoites enlarge to become trophozoites, feeding on the substance of the red cells as they do so. The trophozoites then begin to divide repeatedly to form merozoites, a process called erythrocytic schizogony. The resulting schizont ruptures into the blood stream releasing merozoites, and further invasion of red cells by merozoites occurs (see *Figure 5.1* on page 78).

The rupture of red cells and the subsequent release of merozoites is accompanied by bouts of fever. In the case of P vivax and P ovale this occurs at intervals of approximately three days. With P malariae it occurs about every fourth day and with P falciparum every third day or less. In the case of vivax, ovale and malariae malaria, rupture of red cells takes place in the peripheral blood but in the case of falciparum malaria it takes place in capillaries deep in the tissues. This is responsible for the widespread damage to organs such as the

Figure 5.1: The life cycle of the malaria parasite

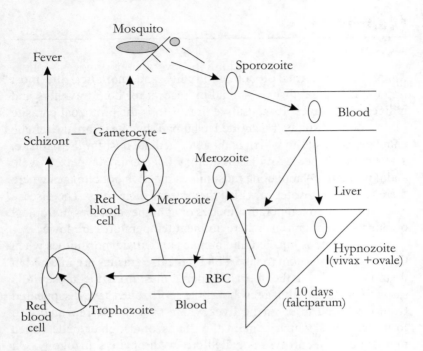

gut, brain, kidneys, liver and lungs, as seen in this type of malaria.

Some of the merozoites do not form schizonts in red cells but develop into gametocytes which carry out the sexual phase of the life cycle of the parasite. Male and female gametocytes are ingested by the female mosquito in which they mature and unite to form oocysts. These in turn rupture to release sporozoites which find their way to the mosquito's salivary glands ready to infect another human host.

Some of the sporozoites entering the liver may become dormant. They are then known as hypnozoites. After a period of time, which may vary from days to months, the hypnozoites become activated and the liver and blood stages of the life cycle then begin. This phenomenon explains why vivax, ovale and malariae malaria may have a long initial incubation period and why relapses may occur. Falciparum malaria, which does not produce hypnozoites, has a shorter incubation period and does not have a tendency to relapse.

Clinical features of malaria

The principal initial symptom is fever which may be accompanied by rigors. Typically the fever is said to have three stages: a cold stage, when shivering or rigors occur and the temperature rises, a hot stage when the temperature remains high for several hours, and a sweating stage when profuse sweating occurs and the temperature begins to fall. After about a week the fever may fall into a typical pattern of waxing and waning every three days, though this is not always seen, especially in falciparum malaria. Falciparum malaria in particular is dangerous, and potentially fatal if not rapidly diagnosed and treated, as extensive multi-organ damage may occur due to obstruction of capillaries by infected, damaged and destroyed red cells. Jaundice and enlargement of the spleen (an early sign) and anaemia due to haemolysis may be seen in all types of malaria. In the case of falciparum malaria, diarrhoea due to damage to the gastrointestinal tract, confusion, coma and convulsions due to cerebral damage, pulmonary oedema, renal and hepatic failure may also occur.

If a traveller who has returned from a malarial area *within the last six to twelve months* develops fever, whether or not anti-malarial drugs have been taken, malaria must not be excluded. Many episodes of malaria have initially been diagnosed as influenza through failure to consider the possibility of malaria or failure to take an adequate travel history, sometimes with fatal results. All travellers to malarial areas should be warned before travelling to ensure that any fever during their travels, or within six to twelve months of their return, is investigated as possible malaria. Some considerations include:

- always asking a patient with an undiagnosed fever if he/she has been abroad in the last six months or more
- requesting an urgent blood film for malaria if the patient has travelled to an area where there is any risk of malaria
- suspecting malaria in the feverish patient with diarrhoea
- suspecting malaria in the feverish patient with jaundice.

Investigation of malaria

The most important means of diagnosing malaria is the identification of malaria parasites in the peripheral blood. It is not essential to wait until the height of the fever to take blood for testing. Thick and thin films are usually requested. The thick film shows larger numbers of blood cells per field and is therefore more likely to show the presence of parasites in the cells, whereas the thin film makes identification of the type of parasite easier. In travellers from non-malarial countries the presence of parasites is diagnostic of malaria but in indigenous people with some degree of immunity to malaria, parasites may be present in the blood in the absence of clinical disease. It is extremely important to understand that one negative film does not exclude malaria. If there is clinical doubt, repeated films must be examined.

Treatment of malaria

A detailed account of treatment is beyond the scope of this book. Self-treatment courses for travellers will be mentioned later, in the section on anti-malarial drugs.

Immunity to malaria

Immunity to malaria is only likely to occur in indigenous populations who have repeated exposure to infection. Expatriates are unlikely to achieve immunity as it takes ten to fifteen years of repeated exposure to develop. Immunity soon wanes and UK immigrants from malarial countries are at risk if they return to their home countries, though they may not see a need for any precautions.

Malaria in pregnancy and childhood

Children and pregnant women are particularly prone to malaria which may be particularly severe and rapid in its progression.

Malaria prevention

Drug prophylaxis

Prophylactic regimens for adults

No drug resistance		
Drug	**Dose**	**Strength/tablet**
chloroquine *or*	2 tablets weekly	150 mg (base)
proguanil	2 tablets daily	100 mg

Low levels of chloroquine resistance		
Drug	**Dose**	**Strength/tablet**
proguanil *plus*	2 tablets daily	100 mg
chloroquine	2 tablets weekly	150 mg (base)

Chloroquine-resistant falciparum malaria		
Drug	**Dose**	**Strength/tablet**
mefloquine	1 tablet weekly	250 mg
pyrimethamine/ dapsone (Maloprim) *plus*	2 tablets weekly	12.5/100 mg
chloroquine	2 tablets weekly	150 mg (base)
doxycycline	1 tablet daily	100 mg

Doses for children

Age	Weight	Fraction of adult dose		
		Chloroquine +Proguanil	Maloprim (Pyr/Daps)	Melfloquine
0–5 weeks		1/8	not rec.	not rec.
6 weeks		1/4	1/8	not rec.
1–5 years	10–15 kg	1/2	1/4	not rec. < 2 yrs or < 15 kg 1/4 (2–5 years)
6–11 years	20–39 kg	3/4	1/2	1/2 (2–5yrs) 1/2 (6–8yrs) 3/4 (9–11yrs up to 45 kgs)
>/=12 years	>40 kg	adult dose	adult dose	adult dose

Standby treatment for adults away from medical facilities for one week

Regimen	Strength/tablet	Dose
Fansidar (pyrimethamine/ sulfadoxine)	25/500 mg	3 tablets in one dose
quinine *plus* Fansidar	300 mg quinine	quinine: 2 tabs 3 times a day x 3 days followed by 3 tabs of Fansidar in 1 dose
quinine *plus* doxycycline	300 mg 100 mg	quinine: 2 tabs 3 times a day x 3 days plus 1 tab of doxycycline twice a day for 7 days
chloroquine	150 mg (base)	4 tabs on days 1 and 2; 2 tabs on day 3

Malaria prophylaxis by region and country

(Information compiled from UK Guidelines, Bradley and Warhurst, 1997)

North Africa and the Middle East

Country	Preferred regimen	Alternative regimen
Very low risk:		
Abu Dhabi	avoid bites	
Algeria		
Egypt (tourist areas)		
Libya		
Morocco		
Tunisia		
Turkey (most tourist areas)		

North Africa and the Middle East continued

Country	Preferred regimen	Alternative regimen
Low risk:		
Azerbaijan (south border areas)	chloroquine	proguanil
Egypt (El Fayum, June to October)		
Iraq (rural north, May to November		
Syria (north border, May to October)		
Turkey (around Adona, Side, SE Anatolia, March to November)		
Tajikistan (south border areas)		
Risk present + chloroquine Resistance		
Afghanistan (below 2000 m, May to November)	chloroquine + proguanil	
Iran (March to November)		
Oman		
Yemen		
UAE (rural north only)		
Saudi Arabia (except north, central and east provinces, Asir plateau and west border cities where risk is very small)		

Sub-Saharan Africa

Country	Preferred regimen	Alternative regimen
Very high risk or locally very high. Widespread chloroquine resistance		
Angola, Benin	mefloquine	chloroquine + proguanil
Burkina Faso		
Burundi		
Cameroon		
Central African Republic		
Chad, Comoros		
Congo, Djibouti		
Eritrea		
Equatorial Guinea		
Ethiopia		
Gabon, Gambia*	*Costal resorts in Kenya and	
Ghana, Guinea	Tanzania for short stays (two weeks	
Guinea-Bissau	or less), and Gambia January to	
Ivory Coast	May: chloroquine and proguanil	
Kenya*	may be used, but protection is	
Liberia	incomplete. Mefloquine for longer	
Madagascar	stays, higher risk activities, for	
Malawi, Mali	example rural trips, safaris,	
Mozambique	backpacking and for Gambia, June	
Niger, Nigeria	to December	
Principe		
Rwanda		
Soa Tome		
Senegal		
Sierra Leone		
Somalia, Sudan		
Swaziland		
Tanzania*, Togo		
Uganda, Zaire		
Zambia		

Sub-Saharan Africa continued

Country	Preferred regimen	Alternative regimen
Risk in some parts. Some chloroquine resistance		
Botswana (north half, November to June)	chloroquine + proguanil	mefloquine *or* Maloprim
Mauritania (all year in south, July to October in north)		
South Africa (north east, low altitude parts of north and east Transvaal, east Natal down to 100 km, north of Durban)		
Zimbabwe (below 1200 m, November to June, all in Zambezi valley where mefloquine is preferred)		
Low risk		
Cape Verde	avoid bites	
Mauritius (except rural areas where chloroquine is appropriate)		

Oceania

High risk. Chloroquine resistance high

Country	Preferred regimen	Alternative regimen
Papua New Guinea (below 1800 m)	doxycycline	mefloquine *or* Maloprim + chloroquine
Solomon Islands		
Vanuatu		

South Asia

Country	Preferred regimen	Alternative regimen
Risk variable. Chloroquine resistance moderate		
Bangladesh (except east; no risk in Dhaka) Bhutan (south only) India (no risk in mountain areas in north) Nepal (below 1300 m; no risk in Kathmandu) Pakistan (below 2000 m) Sri Lanka (no risk in and just south of Colombo)	chloroquine + proguanil	will vary locally
High risk. Chloroquine resistance high		
Bangladesh (only east including Chittagong Hill tract)	mefloquine	chloroquine + proguanil

South-East Asia

Country	Preferred regimen	Alternative regimen
Risk very low — remember if fever		
Bali	avoid bites	
Brunei		
China (main tourist areas)		
Hong Kong		
Malaysia (except Sabah where mefloquine is to be used and deep forests where C + P should be used)		
Sarawak		
Thailand (Bangkok and main tourist areas)		
Risk substantial. Drug resistance common		
Cambodia	mefloquine	
China (only in Yunnan and Hainan; chloroquine in other remote areas)		
Irian Jaya		
Laos		
Myanmar (Burma)		
Vietnam (no risk in cities, Red River delta coastal plain north of Nha Trang)		

South-East Asia continued

Country	Preferred regimen	Alternative regimen
Risk variable. Some chloroquine resistance		
Indonesia (except Bali and cities where risk is low) Irian Jaya (mefloquine) Malaysia and Sarawak (deep forests of the peninsular) Philippines (rural areas below 600 m; no risk in Cebu, Leyte, Bohol, Catanduanes) Sabah	chloroquine + proguanil	
High risk. Mefloquine resistance prevalent		
Cambodia (west provinces) Thailand (borders with Cambodia and Myanmar)	doxycycline	

Duration of drug prophylaxis

Anti-malarials must be started at least one week before entering a malarial area in order to ensure adequate levels in the blood on arrival. They must be continued for four weeks after leaving the area. Failure to observe these rules may result in the development of malaria, even if the drugs have been taken throughout the stay.

Side effects of anti-malarial drugs, contra-indications and cautions

Chloroquine and proguanil

Both drugs may be taken during pregnancy, but chloroquine should not be taken by those with a history of epilepsy. Both drugs may be associated with hair loss.

Mefloquine

Mefloquine may be taken in the second and third trimesters of pregnancy and, like chloroquine, it is not suitable for those with a history of epilepsy. Neuropsychiatric side effects such as depression, nightmares, hallucinations, psychosis and convulsions have been reported. They are not common events, having been reported with a frequency of only 0.01 per cent (Steffen *et al*, 1993), though recent experience suggests that this figure may actually be higher. There is also a possibility of unsteadiness or dizziness. Most of these effects occur very early, often within the first three doses. It is therefore advisable to start treatment with mefloquine three weeks before departure so as to 'weed out' those who develop side effects, stop the drug and substitute an alternative choice of drug. It should be stressed that taking mefloquine carries a much lower risk than does falciparum malaria itself, which may be fatal.

Doxycycline

Like all tetracyclines, doxycycline may cause photosensitive skin eruptions on exposure to sunlight. Because of the deposition of tetracyclines in bones and teeth it is not suitable for use in pregnancy or childbirth. It may be started a day or two before departure but needs to be continued for four weeks after exposure.

Non-drug prevention

If no infected mosquitoes are allowed to bite an individual, malaria will not occur. Avoidance of bites is of prime importance as no regime of drug prophylaxis is one hundred per cent effective. Both methods are of importance, however, as avoidance cannot be relied upon one hundred per cent either.

Covering up

Malaria-carrying mosquitoes bite from dusk to dawn. Between these times it is advisable to keep as much as possible of the skin surface covered with clothing. Mosquitoes and flies carrying other diseases may bite during daylight, and similar precautions may be needed by day if this is a local risk.

Insect repellents

When at risk from mosquito or other bites, areas of skin that cannot be covered should have an insect repellent applied to them. The most effective repellent is DEET which should be used in a concentration of at least twenty to thirty per cent and up to fifty per cent in heavily infested areas. It may be applied as liquid, cream, gel, solid stick or spray. It should not be applied close to the eyes and may damage some fabrics and plastics such as spectacle frames. Applications should be repeated at intervals as directed by the manufacturers and after swimming. One hundred per cent DEET is too highly irritant for direct use on the skin but may be used to impregnate clothing such as socks, neckerchiefs and wristbands that can then be used to protect partially exposed areas.

Mosquito nets

Sealed air-conditioned hotel rooms should offer protection against entry by mosquitoes. Mosquito screens on doors and windows may not be effective or may not fit properly, or there may be gaps around window frames. If there is any doubt about the effectiveness of screening, or if none exists, a mosquito net of sufficiently small mesh size should be used over the bed. It must be suspended from above by the suspension point(s) provided and its frame, if one is provided, should be erected within it to ensure a correct drape. If the net is not impregnated, the sleeper must not come into contact with it as mosquitoes may then be able to bite through the mesh. The net must be tucked in all the way around the mattress. Before use it must first be checked for holes and, if any are present, they must be repaired or temporarily plugged with, for example, cotton wool. Nets are rendered considerably more effective if first impregnated with the insecticide, permethrin. This may be done by the purchaser but it is easier to buy an already impregnated net. After six months of use, the net needs to be re-impregnated. Permethrin kills mosquitoes on contact and will therefore account for any which land on the net whether or not they are able to penetrate the mesh. There is also evidence that the insecticidal effect of a permethrin-impregnated net will reduce the mosquito population in a room to an extent which offers some protection to other occupants of the room (Curtis, 1999). An impregnated net need not necessarily be tucked in if it reaches completely down to the floor.

Other precautions

Mosquito coils are of variable quality and are not reliable in keeping mosquitoes at bay when burned in a room. Electronic buzzers are completely ineffective, but electric vapourisers that vapourise tablets of insecticide may be effective if electricity supplies are reliable. It is useful to erect the mosquito net, close the doors and windows and spray a knock-down insecticide into the room about half an hour before retiring for the night. If sleeping in a tent it is necessary to use a mosquito net, as mesh built into the tent is seldom effective in keeping mosquitoes out. When sleeping out of doors it will be necessary to find or improvise suspension points for the net.

Self-treatment

In areas where effective drug prophylaxis is difficult to achieve because of multiple drug resistance, or when side effects or contra-indications cause problems in taking drugs, it is acceptable to rely on taking precautions against bites and (especially if remote from medical help) to carry a course of one of the self-treatment regimes (see section on drugs and doses). At the first sign of fever the course is started but it is still important to reach a reliable hospital or clinic as soon as possible after starting treatment. Investigation is still needed and other diseases may possibly be present. If the traveller will be close to reliable medical facilities at all times and is relying solely on anti-mosquito precautions for one of the reasons given above, it may not be necessary to carry a self-treatment course if immediate investigation of fever is possible. Another group of travellers for whom anti-mosquito precautions alone, with or without a self-treatment course, may be necessary is the group of business travellers who may travel to malarial areas for short periods at unpredictable intervals and at short notice, without adequate time to arrange drug prophylaxis or to start it prior to travelling.

It is vital that all those who do not take drug prophylaxis report any fever, not only while abroad but also within six to twelve months of their return from a malarial area. This, of course, applies also to those who have taken prophylaxis. Up to two thousand cases of malaria are imported into the UK each year, with ten or more deaths among them (Bradley and Warhurst, 1997). Most of these cases — and an even higher proportion of the deaths — occur in those who have not taken prophylaxis or have not completed the course of treatment. While drugs may not always prevent infection with malaria parasites they appear to reduce the severity of, and the mortality from, malaria if it does develop. Many cases of malaria are initially misdiagnosed as influenza, and this is more likely to occur if a careful travel history covering the last six to twelve months is not taken from patients who present with an undiagnosed fever.

6

Assessing the risks of travel

Risk assessment

Previous chapters have discussed some of the risks that travellers may run. What is needed now is a means of putting this information together to assess risk for the individual traveller.

Travel risks are not by any means confined to infectious or tropical diseases. The most frequent reason for death or emergency repatriation to the UK is heart disease, with accidents coming second. However, in younger travellers, accidents are the most frequent cause. The most frequent risk for most travellers is that of diarrhoea. When travellers go from a developed to a less-developed country, they have a risk of developing a diarrhoeal illness of around one in two. The most frequently encountered vaccine-preventable infection in travellers, with a risk of about one in three to five hundred is hepatitis A, while the risk of typhoid — against which travellers are often vaccinated — is about one in fifty thousand worldwide, though it is higher in India, Africa and some parts of South America. Unprotected travellers in West Africa have a risk of about one in a hundred of developing malaria, but the risk is much lower in many other malarial countries.

Figure 6.1 on *page 96*, based on data from Steffen and Lobel (1996), shows on a logarithmic scale the risks per month of exposure of some travel-associated health risks and other health-related events. It is against this background of the relative frequency with which health risks occur that advice to travellers should be set.

The figures along the baseline refer to the relative risk of developing travel-associated diseases per month of exposure. A relative risk of 1.0 would indicate that all individuals would develop the condition; 0.1 would represent a one in ten risk; 0.01 a one in a hundred risk, and so on. *Note*: the level of risk given for 'bite (risk of rabies)' represents the level of risk of a bite with a potential risk of rabies, and not the risk of acquiring rabies, which would be some-where at the far left of the diagram.

Figure 6.1: Levels of risk for travellers

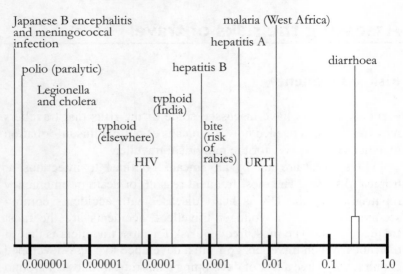

The following factors need to be taken into account when carrying out a risk assessment:

- causes of travel-related disease
- geographical patterns of disease
- age and sex of the traveller
- previous medical history
- itinerary within the country
- time of travel
- method of travel
- length of stay
- type of accommodation
- activities during the stay.

Causes of travel-related disease

See *Chapter 1* for an account of the causes and transmission of common travel-related health problems for travellers. Conditions such as contamination of food and water, sanitation, general hygiene, public health and climate are to a certain extent geographically determined, but not necessarily by national boundaries. A country's climate, socio-economic status and such infrastructure as water supply and sanitation are important determinants of the risk to travellers, and these factors produce a greater number of similarities than differences between developing countries in terms of the health risks found within their boundaries. Poor road conditions, low standards of vehicle maintenance and of driving, and less rigid standards of safety in other areas of public life are further risk factors which do not necessarily depend entirely on geographical location.

Geographical patterns of disease

Although there are important similarities in the health risks to be found in differing geographical locations, there are some risks that are peculiar to some areas, some which are more common in some areas than in others and some which are widely distributed in many countries.

Widespread diseases present in many countries

Poliomyelitis	HIV
Tetanus	Leishmaniasis
Hepatitis A	Dengue fever
Hepatitis B	Filariasis

Widespread diseases found more often in some areas than in others

Typhoid: India, Africa, parts of South America

Diphtheria: former Soviet Union

Meningococcal disease: sub-Saharan Africa, Nepal

P falciparum malaria: sub-Saharan Africa

Schistosomiasis: Africa, Far East

Rabies: India

Onchocerciasis: Africa

Diseases found chiefly in specific areas

Yellow fever: tropical areas of Africa and South America

Japanese B encephalitis: South and South-East Asia

Tick-borne encephalitis: wooded areas of Eastern
Europe and Scandinavia

Trypanosomiasis: sub-Saharan Africa, Central and
South America

Age and sex of the traveller

Elderly travellers

Elderly travellers have reduced reserves of function in all major systems including their immune responses (see *Chapter 3*). They are at increased risk from exacerbations of medical conditions, from thromboembolic disease during travel and from all types of infection.

Children

Children are at increased risk from gastrointestinal infections at many destinations, and from malaria and meningococcal disease at some destinations (see *Chapter 3*). Babies under the age of nine months are not given yellow fever vaccine because of an increased risk of encephalitis, and so may be at risk of infection if taken to endemic areas. Under the age of eighteen months to two years, children do not respond well to meningococcal and Typhoid Vi antigen vaccines. The risk of typhoid infection in children under the age of one year is small and vaccination is not recommended for them, but the risk of meningococcal infection is higher in children than in adults. There is controversy over whether children should be given hepatitis A vaccine. The risk of infection should be balanced against the likelihood of the disease in children being mild and possibly subclinical, with ensuing natural immunity.

Female travellers

The problems that are specific to female travellers are discussed in *Chapter 3*.

Pregnant women and their foetuses

Pregnant women are at increased risk from malaria. However, they are unable to take mefloquine in the first trimester of pregnancy, and the risk of travelling to areas with a high prevalence of chloroquine-resistant falciparum malaria with less effective prophylaxis must be discussed carefully. There is at least a theoretical risk from giving live vaccines to pregnant women. For a pregnant woman travelling to an endemic yellow fever area, the relative risks to her pregnancy of the vaccine and the disease may come out on the side of vaccination if the risk of the disease is very high.

Previous medical history

Problems related to travelling with pre-existing medical conditions have been dealt with in *Chapter 3*. A pre-travel health check and a medication review will help to uncover potential difficulties which can be dealt with as a part of the preparations for travel, such as vaccinations and malaria prophylaxis, the mode or destination of travel and the activities to be undertaken on arrival.

Itinerary within the country

It is important to know not only which countries will be visited, but also the precise areas of those countries. The distribution of malaria is a good example of this. In some countries, such as Thailand, there is a high risk of malaria in some rural areas but a low risk in urban areas or tourist coastal resorts. The distribution of malaria also varies with altitude, being a risk in lowland areas but not in mountainous regions. For example, there is little risk of malaria for the tourist who, travelling to Nepal, flies into Kathmandu and leaves from there to trek into the mountains, but for the trekker who carries on to visit the game parks adjacent to the Indian border there is a definite risk of malaria.

Japanese encephalitis may be a risk for travellers to some parts of South-East Asia, chiefly if they spend time in the rural rice-growing areas rather than travelling to capital cities for business reasons. Similarly, tick-borne encephalitis is unlikely to occur in eastern Europe unless the traveller intends to walk in the forest regions.

Travellers to remote areas may need more advice and protection than other travellers. If they are to be remote from reliable medical facilities, they may be at greater risk of infection with hepatitis B from invasive forms of treatment by less reliable individuals or institutions. In countries where there is a risk of rabies, travellers to remote areas may not have quick or easy access to a source of post-exposure rabies vaccine and, if they are at substantial risk of contact with animals, rabies vaccination should be considered.

Time of travel

There is a variation in the risk of developing some travel-related diseases according to the time of year of the visit. Meningococcal disease, for example, is more likely to occur during the hot, dry season which favours the spread of droplet infection. Conversely, Japanese B encephalitis is more likely to occur in the areas described above during the wet season, when mosquitoes are breeding in the flooded rice paddies.

Method of travel

Air travel carries risks of thromboembolic disease, particularly for the elderly and for travellers with cardiovascular disease or increased susceptibility to clotting. Sufferers from both acute and chronic upper respiratory tract illness may experience acute discomfort in the ears when flying, but most travellers with chronic diseases will be fit to fly unless suffering severe cardiorespiratory impairment. Other aspects of fitness to fly are discussed in *Chapter 2*.

Long-distance travel of any kind may involve the traveller in undergoing prolonged immobility and subsequently an increased risk of thromboembolism. Overland travel in developing countries may introduce the traveller to a wide range of other risks including dust, animals and other allergens, droplet infection, lack of sanitation and poor food and water hygiene, as well as a risk of trauma and subsequent medical treatment in dubious facilities.

The risks of sea travel vary from the hazards of travelling in unseaworthy or overloaded vessels in less well-controlled areas of the world, to trauma from falling down companionways, sunburn and exposure to sexual adventures on cruise ships, together with risks of excessive alcohol consumption which may predispose to all the other risks.

Length of stay

In general, the risk from a particular health hazard, particularly infectious and insect-borne diseases, will rise with an increasing length of stay in the area in which the risk exists.

Tourists on cruises who go ashore for very short periods may be at little risk from most of the health hazards that exist in their port of call. They may be tempted by unwise indulgence in food and drink, but may well be back on board before malaria-carrying mosquitoes begin to bite at dusk. Short-stay tourists — that is, those who spend two weeks or less in a country — may run a risk of hepatitis A from food or water contamination, but the risk to them from insect-borne diseases, such as malaria, may be relatively small, particularly if they travel to comparatively low risk areas of a country. This type of consideration has resulted in a change in the advice on malaria prophylaxis that is given, for example, to short-stay UK tourists in West African coastal resorts to take chloroquine and proguanil, with a lower effectiveness than mefloquine, in view of the side-effect profile of mefloquine.

Longer-term travellers, that is those going abroad for four weeks or more, and expatriate workers will be exposed to health hazards for much longer periods and are thus more at risk from them. They should therefore be offered protection against all the vaccine-preventable diseases they may encounter in the country concerned, as well as being offered appropriate advice on malaria prevention. For the same reasons as those given for travellers to remote areas, it may be appropriate to offer hepatitis B or rabies vaccination, and advice about HIV avoidance is also appropriate.

Type of accommodation

Air-conditioned five-star hotels should be proof against access by mosquitoes during the night, but less well-protected accommodation may need the use of a mosquito net and other precautions in malarial countries. Expensive hotels may appear on the surface to be clean and hygienic, but their ability to pass on food poisoning depends on the personal and professional habits of the staff employed in the kitchen and dining room, which are less apparent to the customer.

The lower the traveller goes down the scale of accommodation the more likely there are to be health risks from a lack of food, water and other hygiene. Where accommodation is shared, as in some 'local-style' hotels and lodges, the more likely is the possibility of droplet infection and the acquisition of diseases of close personal contact, such as diphtheria and meningococcal disease as well as more mundane respiratory infections.

Activities during the stay

Adventure-type holidays involving such activities as mountaineering and white-water rafting carry obvious risks including trauma and drowning. Water sports and swimmimg or bathing may also expose the traveller to risks such as leptospirosis and schistosomiasis as well as to gastrointestinal and other infections.

HIV infection is now a virtually worldwide problem, as indeed are hepatitis B and other sexually-transmitted diseases. Young, unaccompanied males and females are particularly at risk of planned or unplanned sexual encounters and should be warned of the risks and advised about safe sexual practices. Sex tourists (that is those travelling abroad with the intention of having sexual adventures — probably on a commercial basis) are at great risk because sex workers of both sexes have a high prevalence of HIV and other sexually-transmitted infections in countries where sex tourism is common. This group is unlikely to volunteer its intentions and request advice, but the possibility should be borne in mind during travel health consultations.

Travellers going abroad to work as medical, nursing or other aid workers, or as teachers are more at risk from diseases of close personal contact such as diphtheria, meningococcal infection and tuberculosis. Such travellers should be advised about protection against these diseases.

The use of databases in assessing risk

The most frequently used type of database providing travel health information in the primary care setting in the UK is the wall chart, usually culled from one of the popular publications aimed at the primary healthcare team. Such charts can give a great deal of useful information about disease risks in a particular country, but there are problems about keeping the information on them up to date. In addition, it is difficult for a printed chart to contain sufficient information to enable an individual assessment of risk to be made according to the particular circumstances of a traveller's itinerary and activities.

Computer databases have been an obvious development in providing more comprehensive and more specific information. In the UK there are two principal databases in use. 'Travax' is a regularly updated, on-line database maintained by the Scottish Centre for Infection and Environmental Health (see *page 147*). It may be accessed by the use of communications software for an annual fee and has recently been made available on the Internet. 'Traveller' is a software application produced by Microdata I.T. Ltd and supplied on disk for an annual fee that includes monthly update disks. These databases provide not only country-specific information but also information that enables the travel health adviser to consider the risks specific to the individual traveller and his or her particular type of journey. Information on accessing them is given in the *Appendix* on *page 147*.

Even with the use of comprehensive information from databases such as Travax or Traveller, it is still necessary for the travel health adviser to enquire closely into the details of the traveller and his or her journey in order to obtain the relevant information from the database and apply it to the individual traveller using the principles outlined in this chapter (see *Figure 6.2* on *page 104*).

Figure 6.2: Putting it all together — the risk assessment

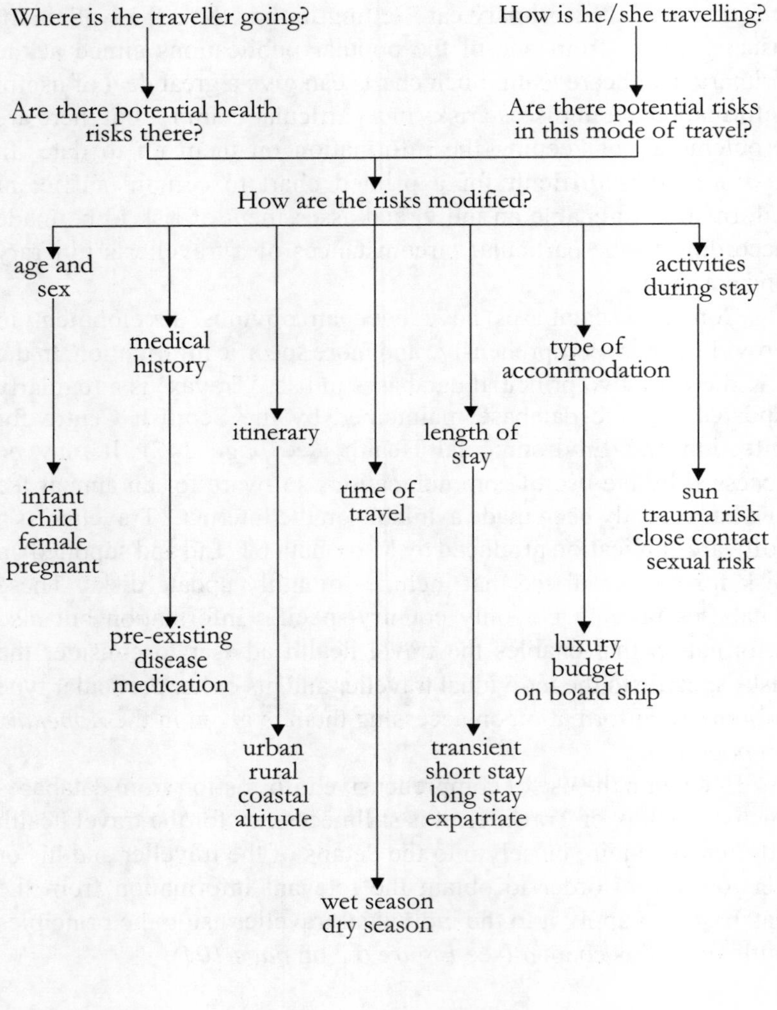

Where is the traveller going?   How is he/she travelling?

Are there potential health risks there?   Are there potential risks in this mode of travel?

How are the risks modified?

- age and sex
- medical history
- itinerary
- time of travel
- length of stay
- type of accommodation
- activities during stay

infant
child
female
pregnant

pre-existing
disease
medication

urban
rural
coastal
altitude

wet season
dry season

transient
short stay
long stay
expatriate

luxury
budget
on board ship

sun
trauma risk
close contact
sexual risk

7

Problems of the returned traveller

The purpose of this chapter is not to produce experts in tropical medicine or to encourage the 'amateur' investigation of patients who should be referred to specialist clinics. Such a practice could prove dangerous. However, it is desirable that the travel clinic, GP or practice nurse should be able to offer simple advice to returning travellers who are ill, investigate and manage certain problems appropriately, and recognise which patients to refer for expert advice, and particularly those who need urgent referral.

The febrile traveller

Travellers who return home with, or subsequently develop a raised temperature may be suffering from a wide range of conditions. Among them is *malaria* which, in the case of P falciparum, is potentially rapidly fatal if not diagnosed early. The investigation of a febrile traveller is therefore an urgent matter, particularly if he or she has recently returned from an area with a high endemicity of falciparum malaria such as sub-Saharan Africa. As P falciparum does not form hypnozoites in the liver, the symptoms of falciparum malaria occur within two months of returning from a malarial area, and often within one month. Blood must be taken as soon as possible for thick and thin films without waiting for the height of fever to occur and, if initially negative, tests must be repeated if a high level of suspicion is present. Malaria parasites are best identified by those used to looking at them, and if there is a high level of suspicion it may be advisable to admit the patient without delay to a specialist unit. The classical periodicity of fever may not be seen in falciparum malaria, and the initial symptoms may suggest a diagnosis of flu. If the patient has classical paroxysmal fever, particularly if the onset of symptoms is delayed beyond one or two months following return, vivax malaria is a more likely diagnosis and presentation may be delayed until between six to twelve months following return home.

Fever with diarrhoea may sometimes be a presenting symptom of malaria, while *typhoid* is initially a febrile illness and not a diarrhoeal one. Symptoms of typhoid usually begin within three weeks of the traveller's return, and the Indian subcontinent is numerically the most likely source of infection for UK travellers. In the absence of any characteristic changes in the differential white cell count in febrile travellers who do not have malaria and have been exposed to a possible risk of typhoid, admission to hospital and the taking of a blood culture will be necessary to exclude typhoid.

Another febrile illness which may suggest flu and may, like flu, go on to cause a cough and pneumonia is *legionnaires' disease*. Diarrhoea may also occur. Infection will usually have occurred within ten days to two weeks of the onset of symptoms, often from air-conditioning or shower heads in hotels. If early treatment with erythromycin is given, the condition may well respond without any of its life-threatening, multi-organ complications and, quite possibly, without the true diagnosis ever being suspected. Serological testing will confirm the diagnosis. Infection is more likely in the elderly and the immunocompromised. There are, of course, many other febrile illnesses which a traveller could bring home, and a systematic approach to the diagnosis of fever is necessary. The following is a suggested proceedure for approaching the problem.

1   Is there an acute fever?
2   Is a malaria film positive?
3   If not, a polymorph count should be the next investigation.
4   If the polymorph count *is not* raised consider:

- viral infection (including dengue; a haemorrhagic rash suggests viral haemorrhagic fever which may include dengue or infections such as Lassa)
- typhoid
- typhus or other rickettsial diseases (there may be a typical eschar at the site of a tick bite).

5   If the polymorph count *is* raised consider:

- are there any symptoms or physical signs suggesting a site of infection? These may include cellulitis or abscesses, localised enlargement such as dysentry, urinary tract infection, and so on

- septicaemia (including meningococcal, which may also have a haemorrhagic rash)
- amoebic liver abscess (may be accompanied by a tender liver)
- Salmonella
- leptospirosis
- legionnaires' disease.

The likelihood of any of the above sources of fever will depend on the itinerary of the traveller and the possibility of exposure to infection. A good travel history is therefore essential. This is by no means a fully comprehensive guide to imported fevers, but serves to illustrate a systematic approach to diagnosis.

Chronic fever

Fevers may be chronic (over two weeks in duration) at the time of presentation, in which case a different range of possibilities presents itself. Once again, a systematic approach is needed, as follows:

1 Does the fever wax and wane? Consider:

- malaria
- filariasis
- leishmaniasis (visceral)
- relapsing fever (borrelia).

2 Is there an increased polymorph count? Consider:

- amoebic liver abscess
- relapsing fever
- deep-seated bacterial infection, for example biliary tract (this may also follow a relapsing pattern).

3 Is there a decreased polymorph count? Consider:

- malaria
- leishmaniasis (visceral)
- widespread tuberculous infection.

4   Is there a normal polymorph count? Consider:
   - localised tuberculous infection
   - trypanosomiasis
   - brucellosis
   - non-infective fever (that is, some other medical condition)

5   Is there a raised eosinophil count? Consider invasive parasitic disease:

   - schistosomiasis
   - filariasis
   - liver fluke
   - visceral larva migrans

Again, this is not a comprehensive guide to chronic and relapsing fevers but illustrates a systematic approach to diagnosis.

Returning travellers who are ill and febrile should ideally be admitted to a specialist unit where a full assessment and appropriate investigations can be carried out.

The traveller with diarrhoea

There is a wide range of possible causes of diarrhoea in the returning traveller, and there are diagnostic pitfalls to be avoided. For example, malaria may present with diarrhoea and valuable time may be lost in awaiting stool cultures. Diarrhoeal diseases do not always conform to a clinical pattern but the following scheme, according to the presence of fever or blood in the stools, will help to focus an investigation.

1   Is there diarrhoea without blood in the stools and without fever? Consider:

   - toxins, for example Staph. aureus or food toxins
   - enterotoxic E coli
   - viral infection
   - Clostridium
   - malabsorption (tropical sprue).

2 Is there fever as well as diarrhoea? Consider:
   - malaria
   - Salmonella
   - Shigella
   - Campylobacter
   - Legionella.

3 Is there blood in the stools as well as diarrhoea? Consider:
   - amoebiasis
   - schistosomasis
   - inflammatory bowel disease, such as ulcerative colitis.

4 Is there blood in the stools and fever as well as diarrhoea? Consider:
   - Shigella
   - Salmonella
   - Campylobacter
   - verotoxic E coli.

5 Are the stools profuse and watery? Consider:
   - cholera.

6 Is there offensive flatus and belching? Consider:
   - giardiasis.

7 Investigation of the traveller with diarrhoea should include:
   - microscopy and culture of the stools
   - blood film for malaria
   - white cell count
   - serology for specific causes of diarrhoea according to clinical suspicion and countries visited.

If the patient is systemically ill, if diarrhoea is profuse and debilitating or if there is a substantial risk that malaria may be present, admission to a specialised unit should be sought.

The traveller with jaundice

Causes of jaundice in the returning traveller include:

- Hepatitis A and B
- non-A, non-B hepatitis, for example hepatitis E from India and Nepal, blood-borne hepatitis C
- falciparum malaria
- leptospirosis.

In the case of hepatitis A, the incubation period may be up to six weeks. Initially the patient may suffer non-specific symptoms such as weakness, malaise and flu-like symptoms but with the onset of jaundice he or she is often feeling much better. The incubation period of hepatitis B is much longer — up to six months — and clues may be obtained from a history of sexual contact, dubious medical treatment, needle sharing by drug users, body piercing or tattooing. If the patient is ill at the time of jaundice, hepatitis A is less likely and malaria is much more likely. Leptospirosis may occur from time to time in those who have been exposed to risk during water sports. Investigation of the jaundiced traveller should include:

- blood film for malaria
- white cell count
- liver function test
- serology for hepatitis.

Once again, systemically ill patients, or those with a substantial risk of malaria, should be admitted to a specialist unit.

The traveller with a skin rash

Possible causes of a skin eruption in the returning traveller include:

- insect bites, with or without secondary infection. These are found mostly on exposed skin areas and are particularly common around the ankles. They are often papular but may be surrounded by spreading erythema and may be disguised by scratching or infection
- cutaneous larva migrans. Here the lesions consist of irregular and intensely itchy tracks in the skin caused by the wanderings of canine hookworm larvae that gain access to the wrong host by contact of human skin with dog faeces, usually in soil or on beaches

- erythema chronicum migrans is the initial skin lesion of Lyme disease. An erythematous reaction spreads outwards from the site of the initial tick bite. The infection may at a later stage affect the heart, joints or central nervous system
- slowly-progressing ulcerated lesions on exposed areas of skin may be caused by cutaneous leishmaniasis acquired from sandfly bites
- if the traveller has been bathing or swimming in fresh water, especially in Africa, an itchy papular rash may be swimmer's itch, the initial skin lesion of schistosomiasis
- bizarre rashes, sometimes appearing to run in swathes down the skin, may be caused by contact with toxic plant juices
- filariasis may cause recurrent episodes of lymphangitis which may be accompanied by fever
- blind boils may result from infestation of the skin by the larvae of the tumbu fly.

Investigation of the traveller with a rash will depend upon the clinical suspicions aroused by the appearance of the rash.

The traveller with respiratory symptoms

Many travellers presenting with respiratory symptoms will simply have acquired viral respiratory infections from close contact with fellow travellers on buses, trains or aircraft. A sore throat may, however, be a warning of diphtheria in travellers from former Soviet Union countries and elsewhere, or of viral haemorrhagic fevers such as Lassa in travellers from Africa. Pneumonia has already been referred to in the context of legionnaires' disease which may also affect other organ systems, including the central nervous system.

The traveller with neurological symptoms

Symptoms such as delirium, confusion, hallucinations or impaired consciousness indicate serious systemic disease. Malaria, typhoid and legionnaires' disease are among the possible causes.

Post-travel screening

There is usually little to be gained by screening returned travellers who have no symptoms. Virtually all of the infections that they could have acquired are likely to produce symptoms which would lead the traveller to seek advice. Some travellers, however, may have specific anxieties about possible exposure to specific infections. A traveller who has been bitten by an animal may, with some reason, be concerned about the possibility of rabies, and the safest course of action in such a case is to give a post-exposure course of rabies vaccine. Some travellers may be worried about the possibility of having intestinal parasites and then stool microscopy, perhaps with an eosinophil count in the case of strongyloides, will help to identify their presence. A raised eosinophil count may also help to suggest the presence of schistosomiasis in those who have been exposed to the risk while travelling in Africa and feel unwell, but serology will also be needed. Finally, there may be anxiety about the possibility of HIV infection if there is a history of potentially unsafe sexual encounters, or medical treatment in dubious surroundings. It is important to give appropriate counselling before testing for HIV and to make allowances for the period of three months before serological testing becomes positive following exposure.

Treatment of the returned traveller

For the inexperienced, it is advisable to discuss the treatment of any condition diagnosed with a tropical or infectious disease specialist. There may be other conditions present in addition to those diagnosed which also need investigation or treatment. The *British National Formulary* (Mehta, 1998) gives a useful guide to the treatment of malaria, and indeed to the treatment of other tropical diseases.

8

Setting up a travel service in the practice

Do we need a travel clinic?

Giving the patients of the practice a travel health service does not necessarily imply setting up a clinic. Like good asthma and diabetes care it is the quality of service given to patients and not the mere presence of a clinic that is important. Particularly in small practices, the numbers of travelling patients may not justify setting a whole session of nurse or doctor time aside unless clinics are held relatively infrequently, and then they may not be available when patients need them. There are, however, advantages to be gained by putting time aside for a clinic. These include:

- the doctor or nurse will be in 'travel mode' and ready to answer patient enquiries
- equipment needed for travel consultations will be immediately to hand
- adequate time can be given to each patient
- access to computer databases can be arranged in advance of the clinic
- travel-associated goods and medical kits can be displayed for sale to patients.
- patients may be attracted in from other practices that do not offer an organised travel service.

How do we investigate the need for a clinic?

A simple audit of travel-associated consultations with all members of the practice team will demonstrate the number of patients likely to attend a clinic over a given period of time. The frequency of clinics and the number of appointments likely to be needed per session can then be calculated. The audit may need to be carried out at more than one time of the year as the demand for travel advice is likely to be seasonal, though there is no close season for travel as the number and variety of holiday and business destinations proliferates.

What do I need to set up a clinic?

The requirements for setting up a clinic include:

- **a room:** a consulting room or treatment room with a couch, desk and chairs and a table or other facility to display travel kits and information leaflets would be the basic minimum needed
- **a vaccine refrigerator:** with an externally displayed maximum/minimum thermometer, no ice box and used only for vaccines (and possibly for other injectable drugs, but not for food and drinks) and fitted with a lock. For information on where to obtain advice about suitable models see the *Appendix, page 147*
- **equipment for injections:** including syringes and needles suitable for intramuscular, subcutaneous and intradermal injections
- **resuscitation equipment:** for use in the unlikely event of an anaphylactic reaction, including a pre-loaded syringe of 1/1000 adrenaline, antihistamine and hydrocortisone injections, oxygen, a nebuliser and bronchodilator nebuliser solution, and equipment for maintaining an airway
- **databases and information sources:** the HMSO publications on Immunisation against Infectious Disease (the 'Green Book', DoH, 1996a) and Health Information for Overseas Travel (the 'Yellow Book', DoH, 1998a) and the *British National Formulary* (Mehta, 1998) are essential and should be supplemented by a computer database such as Travax or Traveller (see *page 147*)
- **communications equipment:** the clinic should have immediate access, preferably in the same room, to a computer for access to databases and for recording patient contacts, and also to a telephone with an outside line for consulting specialist information sources
- **an appointments system:** because of the sometimes complex nature of travel consultations, an appointments system is

desirable to ensure that adequate time is available for each patient

- **trained staff:** reception staff need to be trained to run the clinic effectively. The doctor and/or nurse running the clinic need training and experience in travel health and risk assessment. It is not acceptable for a doctor to delegate all responsibility for travel health to an untrained nurse with no more access to information than a chart culled from an old copy of one of the medical magazines
- **policies and protocols:** the aims of the travel clinic must be clear and must be translated into policies of which all members of the practice team are aware. The policies must be accompanied by protocols by which those policies will be put into operation.

Becoming a Yellow Fever Vaccination Centre

Yellow fever vaccine may only be administered in a Yellow Fever Vaccination Centre, but it is a simple procedure to set up a Centre and any practice may apply to become a Centre. The regulations are as follows:

- the Centre must be under the direction of a registered medical practitioner
- vaccine storage and administration procedures must conform to current standards of practice. A vaccine refrigerator with an externally visible thermometer must be used, but this should be standard procedure for the storage of all vaccines
- the yellow fever vaccine used must be obtained from an approved supplier and be of a quality approved by the World Health Organization (WHO)
- the vaccine must be given by the registered medical practitioner in charge of the clinic, a partner, or a nurse acting under his instructions but not necessarily in his presence
- an International Certificate of Vaccination must be completed in a form which complies with WHO regulations, bearing the name and signature of the person being vaccinated, the date, the name, qualifications and signature of the person giving the vaccination

and the manufacturer and batch number of the vaccine used
- a rubber stamp in the accepted format must be applied to the certificate on completion
- a record must be kept of all vaccinations carried out.

Whether the patient is an NHS patient of the practice or not, fees are payable for the vaccination, for the supply of the vaccine and for the certificate. These fees are generally combined into a single fee, usually in the region of £20 to £25. The cost of the vaccine to the practice is in the region of £12.50 per dose.

An application to become a Yellow Fever Vaccination Centre should be made to the Department of Health. The addresses for application in England, Scotland, Wales and Northern Ireland are listed in the *Appendix*.

Charging for vaccinations and other items

There are two types of payment for travel vaccinations. These are:

- reimbursement for the supply of the vaccine
- the fee for administering the vaccine and taking the responsibility for its administration.

Vaccine supply and reimbursement

The position regarding obtaining and gaining reimbursement for travel vaccines is often confusing and has changed a little recently. The following information embodies current advice in 1999 from the Prescription Pricing Authority (PPA) and a number of Health Authority sources:

1   Vaccines that may be purchased and reimbursed by means of a bulk claim to the PPA, or prescribed to the patient on an FP10:

- typhoid
- tetanus
- hepatitis A
- hepatitis B
- meningococcal A + C

- influenza
- pneumococcal
- cholera (not currently recommended or available in the UK).

These vaccines may be purchased by the practice (see *Appendix, pages 159 – 160*) and administered to patients, and their cost reclaimed in bulk on Form FP34D. It is not necessary to submit an FP10 prescription for each dose. With the exception of influenza and pneumococcal vaccines, they are widely used for travel purposes. The practice makes a profit on these vaccines by receiving the dispensing fee, an on-cost allowance and the container fee as paid to pharmacists. They may be prescribed on an FP10 given to the patient, but practices with a travel clinic usually prefer to keep vaccines in stock and make a profit on them.

2 Vaccines that are supplied free of charge by the Health Authority:

- poliomyelitis
- diphtheria (including adult diphtheria vaccine).

These vaccines are supplied by the Health Authorities free of charge to GPs as part of their child immunisation policy, and may also be used for travel purposes. Diphtheria and tetanus vaccine for adults (Td) is available free of charge from the Health Authorities in ampoule form, but not in pre-filled syringe form. In this form it should be purchased and then reimbursement claimed by submission of an FP10 to the PPA. The free ampoules of Td should not be used for travellers as they are for use in the UK child immunisation schedule.

3 Vaccines reimbursible on an FP10 for some travellers:

- rabies.

Some Public Health Laboratories are able to supply rabies vaccine free of charge for high risk groups (specified in the 'Red Book', note 6 to paragraph 27 of the Statement of Fees and Allowances). Such groups include laboratory workers exposed to a risk of rabies and some veterinary workers and inspectors. Otherwise, the vaccine may be purchased and the cost reclaimed, with the usual additions, by submitting an FP10 to the PPA for these high risk groups, but other travellers should bear the cost of the vaccine themselves.

4   Non-reimbursible vaccines:

- Japanese B encephalitis
- tick-borne encephalitis.

(These vaccines were formerly reimbursed by the submission of an FP10 to the PPA but are no longer reimbursible and must be paid for by the recipient or obtained from a pharmacist by the issue of a private prescription.)

- rabies (for most travellers)

(With the exceptions noted above, travellers must bear the cost of this vaccine themselves.)
Vaccines where the cost is normally reimbursed by the NHS cannot be reclaimed from the PPA by bulk claim or FP10 prescription if they are given to non-NHS patients in the travel clinic. The cost of vaccines for such patients must be passed on to the patient. A profit margin may be added.

5   Yellow fever vaccine.
This is made available only to registered Yellow Fever Vaccination Centres, though any practice or travel clinic may apply to become a Centre. It is purchased and the cost passed on to the patient along with the vaccination fee and the fee for the International Vaccination Certificate, usually set at an all-in fee of about £20 to £25.

Vaccination fees

Vaccination fee claimable on form GMS4

A claim on form GMS4 may be made for administering these vaccines to patients temporarily or permanently registered with the practice. In an increasing number of practices these claims are now made electronically by Item of Service Links without using a GMS4. There are two levels of fee: A and B which, in 1999 are set at £4.30 and £6.25 respectively:

• poliomyelitis	1st and 2nd	A
	3rd and booster	B
• tetanus	1st and 2nd	A
	3rd and booster	B
• typhoid	1st and 2nd	A
	booster	B
• hepatitis A*	one dose only	B
• cholera**	1st and 2nd	A

* Regulations refer to immunoglobulin. Some Health Authorities may pay differently for the vaccine, others may treat it in the same way.

** Not currently available or advised in the UK.

Vaccination fees payable by the patient

A fee of £23.00 is recommended in 1999 by the British Medical Association, and may be charged to the patient for all other vaccinations not claimable on form GMS4, whether the course consists of one or more doses. These include:

• hepatitis B solely for travel purposes
• meningococcal A + C
• Japanese encephalitis
• tick-borne encephalitis
• rabies (for most travellers).

Yellow fever vaccination has already been referred to in detail above. Patients not registered with the practice may be charged a fee of £23.00 for administration of all vaccines, including those for which a GMS4 claim would otherwise be made.

The only vaccination certificate that is required by international regulation is for yellow fever. If a patient requests a certificate for any other vaccination, a fee of £8.00 is appropriate.

Other sources of income

When patients attend your travel clinic they may generate other sources of income.

Prescriptions

Anti-malarial drugs should not be prescribed on an FP10 prescription. Chloroquine and proguanil can and should be purchased over the pharmacy counter, but mefloquine is a Prescription Only Medicine (POM) and needs a private prescription for which a fee of £8.00 is payable to the practice, in addition to whatever the pharmacist charges for the drugs themselves. This prescription fee also applies to other POMs, such as doxycycline, which may occasionally be used for malaria prophylaxis, and other medications which patients may wish to carry against the possiblity of illness while abroad. The NHS does not cover the supply of such items. Simple analgesics, rehydration sachets and antidiarrhoeals, such as loperamide, are available over the counter but if patients wish to carry POMs, for example antibacterial drugs or drugs to combat high altitude problems, then a private prescription, again for a fee of £8.00, should be issued.

Selling travel related goods

The supply of travel-related goods is not covered by the National Health Service and it is possible for a practice operating a travel clinic to supply goods to patients and make a charge for them. Such items include:

- insect repellents
- mosquito nets
- water purifying equipment
- sun screen preparations
- sterile travel/first aid kits.

Sterile kits for avoiding the risk of dirty or re-used equipment for invasive treatments may include syringes, needles, skin sutures, alcohol wipes, sterile gauze swabs and sterile wound dressings. An intravenous giving set and cannula may also be included, and a printed list of contents bearing the name and rubber stamp of the clinic may convince suspicious customs or immigration officials that the contents are bona fide medical equipment. Such kits may be bought in bulk and sold at a profit or made up in the practice in a small zipped bag or sealed plastic box and sold at a price of £10 to £15, depending on their contents.

Travel vaccination in Scottish practices

The position regarding item of service payments is the same in Scotland as it is in the remainder of the UK. The supply of vaccines to the patient does appear to differ, but whether this difference occurs because of long established custom or by regulation is not clear. Most general practices in Scotland appear to give a prescription for the appropriate vaccines that are then dispensed by a pharmacist, the patient then returns to the GP or practice nurse for the injection. There appears to be some confusion over whether Scottish GPs are subject to regulations which prohibit purchase and reimbursement of vaccines, or whether it is simply a matter of historical custom that they do not do so. Guidelines issued by one Scottish Health Board state that all vaccines for which the administration is covered by the GMS4 should be supplied on an NHS prescription dispensed by a pharmacist. All other vaccines may be supplied on a private prescription, charged at the GP's discretion, though there is no regulation that prevents GPs from supplying them on an NHS prescription. If they are prescribed on the NHS, a charge should not be made for administering them, though this is contrary to advice given in England.

Organising your travel clinic

Preparations involved in organising a travel clinic should include:

- deciding who is going to give the vaccinations and agree to sign a protocol for all clinic activities (see *Chapter 9*)
- selecting and maintaining an up-to-date database for vaccination requirements and malaria prevention
- setting up a stock control and ordering policy
- organising a separate travel clinic session if numbers demand it
- displaying a list of services and fees in the wating room and in the clinic
- establishing procedures for:
  - recording what is given and to whom
  - recording fees, billing and issuing receipts

○ completing GMS4 (or instituting an electronic claim)
and FP34D where applicable

○ generating FP10 prescriptions for vaccines where
applicable.

Having set up the procedures, make sure that all practice staff know
how the system operates when patients ask for travel vaccinations or
advice. The travel clinic should be advertised in the practice waiting
room and, where appropriate, patients should be encouraged to
attend. If your practice establishes regular travel clinic sessions or
becomes a registered Yellow Fever Vaccination Centre you may
advertise in local travel agencies.

9

Policy and travel health protocols in practice — *Karen Howell*

Introduction

Primary care continues to be the principal focus for National Health Service policy, with an increasingly pivotal role within the health service. Economic factors have been the major driving force behind strategies to maximise efficient and effective use of National Health Service resources, while delivering a quality-assured standard of healthcare. The introduction of recent health service policies (DoH, 1997 and 1998a) reveals a shift to improve the quality of healthcare with cost-effectiveness still remaining a necessary factor.

At the practice level, this enables the primary healthcare team to improve their clinical effectiveness. It promotes using best available evidence, introducing systems to measure and evaluate healthcare, making efficient use of resources, and ensures that healthcare professionals maintain and keep up to date with new developments (NHS Executive, 1996). Clinical effectiveness is clearly dependent, therefore, upon other key areas — information systems, research evidence, education and audit. Together, these key areas assist health professionals to provide a quality healthcare service that is responsive to change, and these attributes are essential for the provision of a travel health service.

The increasing demand for travel health advice has created a rapidly-expanding service area within primary care that is becoming increasingly complex with changing travel trends. It is a diverse speciality, where advice is dependent upon many factors:

- environmental and geographical conditions
- disease and drug resistance patterns
- vaccine developments
- public health infrastructures
- cultural and sociopolitical circumstances
- assessment of the lifestyle and likely behaviour of travellers.

The provision of travel health advice requires health professionals both to acquire knowledge and to establish dependable resources for information as well as the means to keep up to date with new developments.

Travel health is a relatively new speciality and there is, therefore, a lack of research evidence. Epidemiology provides the main source of reliable data, while other information is obtained from expert opinion, drug manufacturers, personal experience and anecdote. The result is a tendency for travel health information to be conflicting and ambiguous in nature. Consideration of both the diversity within travel health and the lack of research evidence inevitably gives rise to medico-legal concerns amongst health professionals. A prime example of a cause for this fear has been highlighted by the focus of media and legal attention on the anti-malarial drug, mefloquine.

Until travel health becomes fully established as a speciality, with recognised standards of practice and education for healthcare professionals, the quality of travel health advice will be varied. As has been shown in earlier chapters in this book, a travel health service should not be biased solely towards immunisations, but should extend to include risk assessment and health education. Advice should be supported by an evidence base and up-to-date information provided by competent health professionals in travel health. The process of developing a comprehensive travel health service, which is quality driven and meets professional standards of practice, must evolve systematically within a development framework. This framework is provided by a protocol.

The process of developing a travel health service within a protocol framework will promote clinical effectiveness and make efficient use of resources. It facilitates the formation of standards for measurement through audit to ensure that the travel health service remains effective and efficient, responding to the needs of travellers. A protocol does not consider the service alone, but takes into account other factors for its delivery; this includes meeting professional, legal and health service policy demands.

What is a protocol?

Definitions of the terms 'policy', 'guidelines', 'protocol' and 'procedures', and identificaion of their role and logical sequence are provided in *Table 9.1*.

Table 9.1: Definition and sequence of terms	
Term	**Definition**
Policy ⇩	A general course of action setting the direction for detailed planning.
Guidelines ⇩	These are broad statements of action open to interpretation at local levels.
Protocol ⇩	This consists of written recommendations, rules or standards to be followed for any medical situation or service where rational procedures can be specified.
Procedures	These define a precise series of steps to perform a clinical task or to reach certain objectives.

Policies

Policies are developed by organisations for use at international, national, local and practice levels. They reflect the philosophy of an organisation — including compliance with legislation — and act as an 'umbrella', giving the directions. A policy can be written as a general statement of intention or can be specific to a particular issue, such as an alcohol policy.

International policy

The World Health Organization (WHO) plays an important role in developing international health policy by providing guidelines that are subject to governmental interpretation in formulating national policy. For example, the WHO produces annual guidance for travel vaccine requirements and health advice that is principally addressed to national health administrations (WHO, 1999).

The World Tourism Organization (WTO) and the European

Union (EU) have also developed policies affecting travel health. Their significant influence has been through European Law in the form of directives which are incorporated into legislation in this country, becoming a part of national and local policies. For example, an EU Directive for the tourism industry was introduced on package travel, making it an offence for travel operators not to provide their customers with information about health requirements for travel (European Union, 1993). Other EU Directives that affect travel healthcare include employment of health professionals, dealing with hazardous substances and the health and safety of the working environment in which a travel health service is provided.

National Policy

As part of the healthcare service, travel health is subject to general national policies for health, employment, and health and safety at work. Examples of policies directly relating to travel health, are immunisation and communicable disease control. National policy for immunisation is founded upon expert advice from the Joint Committee on Vaccination and Immunisation (JCVI) which is produced in the form of recommendations in *Immunisation Against Infectious Disease* (the 'Green Book', DoH, 1996a). The strength of these recommendations that support policy, compared with other sources of information, is clearly indicated:

> *The recommendations set out in the 'Green Book' are based on the current expert advice available to the Joint Committee on Vaccination and Immunisation (JCVI), although in some circumstances they may differ from that contained in the vaccine manufacturers' data sheets. These recommendations reflect present national immunisation policy.*

Although the publication, *Health Information for Overseas Travel* (the 'Yellow Book') is published by the Department of Health (1995) to complement the immunisation recommendations, the introduction states that it is advisory and is not a statement of government policy.

Local policy

Health Authorities, NHS Trusts and newly-introduced Primary Care Groups are responsible for local healthcare policies. These are developed from national policies, from legislation and from local needs. Policies need to be developed to comply with European Directives, even before they become part of national legislation. Directives have a direct force on state authorities, which includes health authorities and conceivably NHS Trusts, because they are providing a public service under state control with special powers. In principle, this could be applied to Primary Care Groups, depending on their levels of accountability.

The key policy areas for travel health are immunisation, NHS payments for travel vaccines, and communicable disease. NHS payments for travel vaccines and immunisation are subject to local interpretation. This has lead to particular disparity in payments for travel vaccines between health authorities and individual practices. However, local policy has responded to identified local population travel health needs and has sometimes opposed national policy. For example, because of the large number of imported malaria cases amongst its populaton, Lambeth Health Authority decided to make malaria chemoprophylaxis available through the NHS, even though this was in conflict with national policy.

Practice policy

The first question to ask is 'Do you have a practice policy for travel health?' A policy for travel health may exist as part of a general policy of commitment to healthcare services, it may be a separate policy, or it may not exist at all. A policy for travel health will establish the foundation for the development of a travel health service which is specific to such characteristics of the practice as population size, demographics, ethnicity, socioeconomic and travel trends, and healthcare resources.

Careful consideration needs to be given to how a travel health service will be offered to patients. The policy will need to justify providing advice in a designated travel health clinic instead of a sessional or appointment system. A specific travel health clinic implies the existence of a service of expertise. This raises public expectation and increases accountability for the travel health service being provided. Therefore, for its policy in travel health, a practice needs to consider the following factors:

- the practice profile
- healthcare provision
- accountability
- public expectation
- medico-legal implications
- resource allocation.

Guidelines

These can be used in two ways:

1   Giving more detailed information from policies to assist interpretation and implementation at local levels.
2   Providing clinical information from expert opinion and research evidence.

Guidelines are sometimes considered to offer health professionals greater flexibility in making clinical decisions than protocols, but they have different functions which are integral to providing quality travel health advice. A protocol provides the structure in which guidelines are incorporated as supportive evidence for clinical practice.

Protocols

These enable a systematic approach to be developed for providing travel health advice during a consultation. This process is developed within a wider framework that takes into account the following: quality assurance, clinical effectiveness, healthcare resources and professional requirements to implement the service.

Procedures

Procedures break down the components of a protocol into detailed, specific actions undertaken to carry out a function. Clinically they are based upon evidence of good practice and policy, such as immunisation procedures or treatment for anaphylactic shock. The recommendations for immunisation procedures by the Department of Health (DoH, 1996a) include procedures for acquiring appropriate information before immunisation and for the administration of vaccines.

What determines the need for a travel health protocol?

Some fundamental elements underpin the use of a travel health protocol in practice. They are:

- accountability
- medico-legal issues
- national health service policies.

Health professionals who provide a travel health service become responsible and accountable for the service they provide. Having responsibility for giving travel health advice means that health professionals must be satisfied, before undertaking the task, that they possess the required knowledge and competence. The use of the term 'accountability' implies that a situation has been fully assessed, planned and evaluated. Providing travel health advice means taking responsibility for the planning and delivery of the service and, therefore, becoming accountable for the travel healthcare given. Accountability in travel health is multifaceted.

What, then, is a health professional's accountability in travel health? Such accountability includes the following areas:

- personal
- professional
- employer/employee
- traveller
- society.

Personal

We are all individuals who have ethical values that can affect our professional working practice. For example, an area causing some moral discomfort is the public health focus of immunising children against hepatitis A when they are travelling to countries where it is endemic. Part of the rationale supporting this immunisation is to protect the local adult population from exposure to children who return incubating the disease. While hepatitis A is predominantly a mild, transitory illness in children, it is much more serious in adults, causing increased morbidity and mortality.

Professional

For doctors and nurses to practise, they must be registered with the the General Medical Council (GMC) or the United Kingdom Central Council for Nursing, Midwifery and Health Visiting (UKCC). These are self-regulatory bodies which are responsible by law for professional standards. Their main function is to protect the general public by ensuring that both doctors and nurses are professionally accountable and work within the standards of their professional codes of practice. Both regulatory bodies take care to point out that health professionals must be personally accountable for their own professional practice. Clinical governance is being introduced as part of the framework for healthcare service provision to ensure that health professionals remain competent to practise (General Medical Council, 1998).

Employer and employee

Within the structure of primary care, individual health professionals can be classified as an employer or an employee, each class bearing different forms of accountability.

Employers have a duty of care to employees and to travellers using the travel health service. They must delegate responsibilities to competent staff and provide the support required for them to deliver the service for which they are contracted. Their responsibility includes health and safety, ensuring travel health advice is given using good standards of practice in a safe working environment.

Employees are directly accountable to their employer for carrying out a service according to their agreed job description in their contract of employment. Conflict can arise between professional and employer accountabiltiy. For example, a newly-employed practice nurse, with no experience at all in travel health, may be given the responsibility of the travel health service without introductory training. The practice nurse will then be torn between the demands of accountability as a professional and as an employee. Professionally, the practice nurse should refuse the responsibility of giving travel health advice until a satisfactory level of competence is achieved.

Traveller

Healthcare professionals are accountable to travellers for the travel health service they provide. The introduction of the *Patient's Charter* (DoH, 1991) has led to an increasing demand by the general public for their rights in the type of service they receive. Health professionals must be competent to give travel health advice as a service that is developed through consultation with travellers, to meet their needs.

Social

Primary healthcare professionals and Primary Care Groups are increasing their accountabilty for the public health of the community. They are providing services to meet the health needs they have identified for their local population. Travel health has a public health function: the provision of travellers with immunisations and health education also protects the local community at home from communicable diseases brought back by returning travellers.

Medico-legal aspects of travel health

As society becomes more litigious, health professionals' fear of legal action being taken against them grows and can impinge upon their practice. The three main areas in law to consider are:

- criminal law — Medicines Act (1968)
- civil law
- liability.

Criminal law

Health professionals will be affected by criminal law if they commit an offence against a person or become liable through statutory legislation. This applies to laws concerning medicines and health and safety.

Civil law

More commonly, legal action taken against health professionals lies in the domain of civil law, where they are sued for negligence. This occurs when a plaintiff, the person bringing the civil action for harm done, has to prove that the defendant, for example a health professional, was liable. To prove negligence, a plaintiff needs to provide evidence for the following :

1   The health professional had a duty of care.
2   This duty of care was breached.
3   It was reasonably foreseeable.
4   As a consequence, it resulted in harm.

Anecdotally, there have been several reports of health professionals or organisations who provide travel health advice being sued for negligence. Most have been settled out of court amicably. So far, there have been no cases that have set a precedent in law, although there may be an outcome resulting from cases regarding the anti-malarial drug mefloquine.

Liability

There are two types of liability to consider: 'direct' and 'vicarious'. Direct liability occurs when the employer is responsible for error, such as failing to employ a health professional who is competent in travel health and harm has resulted. Vicarious liability means 'indirect liability' and relates to an employer being held responsible for the actions of employees, even though the employer as an individual has done no direct harm.

Medico-legal areas in practice

Travel health practice is affected by many aspects of healthcare law. Some of the main medico-legal areas for individual and professional duty of care are discussed as follows.

Competence to practise

A health professional's competence to practise is judged according to a standard established in a precedent case in law, known as the 'Bolam Test' (1957). The case held that:

> *it is the standard of the ordinary skilled man exercising and professing to have that special skill. A man need not possess the highest expert skill at the risk of being found negligent... it is sufficient if he exercises the skill of an ordinary competent man exercising that particular art.*

Therefore, a health professional's practice will be determined by the standards of professional peers in travel health. They are not required to be experts in travel health, but have adequate knowledge and skills to practise. This part of the law is reinforced by the GMC and UKCC and is an integral part of their respective professional codes of practice.

Delegation

When delegating travel health advice, it is the duty of the person delegating the task to ensure that the health professional carries out that care at a reasonably competent level. The case of Wilsher v Essex AHA (1988) set the standard of reasonable care to be expected of students and junior staff (author's emphasis):

> *The standard is that of a **reasonably competent practitioner**... You have a duty to ensure that the care which you delegate is carried out at a reasonably competent standard.*

In primary care, travel health advice is frequently delegated by doctors to practice nurses. For immunisation, the Department of Health (1996a) has specified the following critera for the delegation of immunisation to nurses, as shown in *Table 9.2* below.

Table 9.2: Criteria for delegation of immunisation to nurses (DoH, 1996a)
A doctor may delegate responsibility for immunisation to a nurse provided:
1 The nurse is willing to be professionally accountable for this work as defined in the UKCC guidelines on the 'Scope of Professional Practice'.
2 The nurse has received training and is competent in all aspects of immunisation, including contra-indications to specific vaccines.
3 Adequate training has been given in the recognition and treatment of anaphylaxis.
Nurses employed by general practitioners should work to agreed protocols including all the above conditions.

There are new initiatives encouraging nurses either into partnerships with doctors in practice, or into taking the lead in providing a service where they employ doctors on a sessional basis. For instance, a practice nurse may set up a travel health clinic and employ a doctor for specific clinic times. In this case, nurses must be equally aware of their legal responsibilities as employers and as professionals in delegating tasks.

Protocols

So far, protocols have not been put to the test in a court of law as evidence for a health professional's practice. However, they are considered by legal experts, professional bodies and unions, to supply written documentation to support the level of care given by a health professional, providing that they are based upon current information. The presence of protocols:

> *shows that healthcare professionals have thought pro-actively about the care they give and there is written evidence of the standard of care.*

(Tingle, 1995)

Group protocol

Travel vaccines are generally administered by nurses using a group protocol agreement, this gives advanced direction and is a practice supported by the UKCC (UKCC, 1993). The legality of using a protocol agreement came into question, as it was not specified in the Medicines Act of 1968. Current practice has evolved beyond the scope of this Act which has been reviewed by the Crown committee (DoH, 1998c). The final report of this committee concerning the supply and administration of medicines, supports the use of a group protocol:

> *for those limited situations where this offers an advantage for patient care, and where it is consistent with appropriate professional relationships and accountability.*

(DoH, 1999)

Due to a diverse interpretation of the term 'group protocol', the Crown committee review team have defined it as follows:

> *A 'Group Protocol' is a specific written instruction for the supply or administration of named medicines in an identified clinical situation. It is drawn up locally by doctors, pharmacists and other appropriate professionals, and approved by the employer, advised by the relevant professional advisory committees. It applies to groups of patients or other service users who may not be individually identified before presentation for treatment.*

(DoH, 1998c)

A group protocol for the administering of travel vaccines should be developed, showing arrangements for professional responsibility and accountability. It should meet the following criteria which are specified by the review committee:

1 Clearly state the clinical need.
2 Detail attributes of health professionals authorised to take responsibility for the supply and administration of travel vaccines under the group protocol.
3 Describe details of the travel vaccines available under a group protocol.
4 Specify the management and monitoring of the group protocol.

Much of the guidance given for these criteria in the Crown Review/ committee is considered in principle for the general development of protocols. Particular note should be taken, however, that an employer is responsible for providing final approval of a protocol in order to ensure full consideration of legal liability and indemnification for staff.

Other areas to consider for professional practice

There are several areas in which health professionals must have greater legal awareness in order to ensure that they are providing a good standard of practice. The main ones to consider are:

- consent
- confidentiality
- standards for record keeping
- health and safety.

National Health Service policies

As explained earlier in this chapter, policies have an impact on travel health practice. Therefore, National Health Service policies play a central role in laying the foundation that underpins the development of a protocol. Some of the main health policy documents to consider include:

- *Primary Care: Delivering the future* (DoH, 1996b)
- *Promoting Clinical Effectiveness* (NHS Executive, 1996)
- *The New NHS: Modern, Dependable* (DoH, 1997)
- *Our Healthier Nation* (DoH, 1998b)
- *A First-Class Service: Quality in the NHS* (DoH, 1998a)

Advantages of a protocol

Advantages for health professionals

Developing a protocol facilitates a multi-disciplinary approach to travel healthcare, where roles and responsibilities are clarified to aid team working. It is helpful in identifying other disciplines, advisory groups and partnerships needing to be involved in the process of development. At the same time it can begin to establish alliances — as advocated in Health Service policy in *The New NHS: Modern, Dependable* (DoH, 1997) — to promote travel health services in primary care; this can be with travel agents, schools, businesses, outdoor shops, and so on.

Collecting information for a protocol supports evidence-based practice. There are many areas in travel health where there are conflicts of medical opinion or dilemmas in practice. Collating data, and consultation, will help health professionals to reach a consensus for the content of a protocol, from which standards can be set and then measured for audit. Health professionals will then be working with the same information and supportive rationale to provide advice to travellers.

Going through the process of developing a protocol clarifies the education and training needs for all the staff involved in providing the travel health service. Having established a protocol, it can then be used as a teaching aid for new members of the travel healthcare team, and becomes an important point of referral for agency staff. It provides support for litigation as well as creating awareness of legal liability between employees and employers. In a more general sense, the development of a protocol facilitates another process in practice; that of risk management, for employers, staff and travellers.

Advantages for the traveller

The use of a written protocol for a travel health service promotes consultation with travellers and the delivery of relevant and uniform information. This will reassure travellers that they are being given quality travel health advice, and will build their confidence in the service being provided. This, in turn, may lead to a traveller being more compliant with the travel health advice given and consequently produce a more successful outcome to their health.

Advantages for the travel health service

The main benefits of a protocol for the travel health service are to improve standards for clinical effectiveness, to make efficient use of resources, to establish a safe system of practice for health professionals and travellers, and to provide a framework for giving travel health advice that includes audit and evaluation.

Disadvantages of a protocol

Although the benefits of a protocol generally outweigh the disadvantages, it is important to identify those areas that may become barriers to developing and implementing a protocol in practice. Members of a travel healthcare team may sometimes view protocols as restricting practice and may find the process of identifying roles and responsibilities threatening to their established position in a practice. It may also be difficult to achieve consensus amongst team members, thus requiring that effort be put into obtaining relevant information.

Another recognised difficulty in protocol development is that it does take time and commitment. The development process should, therefore, work to a systematic plan of action, within a time frame and with tasks delegated to team members. Ensuring that travel healthcare team members are regularly kept up to date with revisions to a protocol may be another hurdle to overcome. A reliable system for informing staff of changes to a protocol needs to be agreed as a part of the implementation process, and a staff member should be designated for the task of updating.

Developing a protocol

There are two principal functions to consider in developing a protocol: how to develop it and how to write it.

How to develop a protocol

The process can be broken down into the following steps.

Organise a working group

Membership of the working group should be multi-disciplinary, so representing all the primary care staff involved in providing the travel health service, for example receptionists, practice nurses, doctors, managers and community pharmacists. Participation by all the key members of the travel healthcare team will give greater ownership of the protocol and thereby improve adherence to its content. Where there are difficulties in arranging a multi-disciplinary group due to personal restraints or lack of motivation, the healthcare professional most active in providing travel health advice should devise a draft protocol. However, working alone on such a document is not easy and requires consultation to reach both consensus and agreement on the protocol's content and use in practice.

Establish an action plan

In order to achieve the goal of a written travel health protocol, an action plan should have a time frame that is practical and realistic. Action points should include the delegation of tasks to each member of the group, with deadlines for completion. Working to such an action plan will make more effective use of the members' time and resources, and will manage the whole process more successfully.

Collect evidence and information

Researching available information and evidence is time consuming. Then follows the process of critical evaluation of the evidence before it is used to support the contents of a protocol.

Consultation

This process should include both individuals outside the working group who are involved in providing travel health services in a practice and those affected by the service, namely travellers. Identify those individuals outside the practice with a professional, public health or service interest in travel healthcare, for example local consultants in infectious disease or genito-urinary medicine, public health doctors and travel agents. All of these groups may bring expertise to different areas in the development of a protocol. At the same time, the process will raise the awareness of interested groups of a travel health service, which may be beneficial to working relationships and improve the standard of travel healthcare in the locality.

Draft formulation

Once the draft is completed, send it to the key individuals identified during consultation. Feedback can be obtained either informally or formally through a questionnaire or interview. There should be a deadline for the completion of feedback.

Consensus and agreement

The working group should consider comments made on the draft and agree their inclusion, if appropriate, in the revised protocol. This stage may require the gathering and use of further evidence to resolve any contentious issues.

Approval of draft

The final protocol should be approved by the local professional advisory group and by the employer for use in the practice.

Implementation

The completed travel health protocol must be dated, read and signed by all the healthcare professionals involved in providing travel health advice, in order to confirm that they have understood the content. Copies can be circulated to the relevant staff and one copy must be available in the setting in which travel health advice is given. Travel healthcare professionals should complete any additional education and training needs in travel health, in accordance with relevant stated professional criteria, before signing the protocol.

The implementation process must include arrangements for monitoring, reviewing and communicating any changes made as a result of new developments in travel health, to ensure that the protocol maintains clinical effectiveness.

How to write a protocol

Write the protocol so that it is clear in direction and can be read easily. This is a step-by-step process. Begin by drafting an outline of the main headings under which the content can be added as it develops. Keep the written information clear, concise and easy to read, following a logical sequence. Remember that the aim is that the protocol can be understood by all staff.

The steps involved in writing a protocol, and which can be used as the initial headings, are as follows.

Step 1: Aims and objectives

At this first stage the demand for travel health advice in a practice should be assessed before deciding on the type of service to be offered, for example a travel clinic, a travel session or *ad hoc* appointments. Providing a travel clinic implies expertise in travel health and may raise travellers' expectations about the quality of service they will receive.

The aim should reflect the general intention of the travel health service to promote the health of travellers and to ensure professional and practice accountability to achieve this goal. The objectives break down this goal into specific areas to make this intention work in practice.

Step 2: Marketing

How will the service be advertised? Will it be through the practice leaflet, posters or the practice newsletter? What about approaching other groups or such organisations as community pharmacists, travel agents or outdoor equipment shops to make them aware of the travel health service? An article in the local newspaper would also raise public awareness of the need to seek advice early and where to go to obtain it.

Step 3: Organisation

This section determines how the service will be planned, setting the scene for the provision of travel health advice. Areas to consider including are:

- appointments
- recall system
- resources
- equipment.

Step 4: Administration

This involves the active running of the travel health service. Areas to consider including are:

- roles and responsibilities
- immunisation group protocol agreement
- record keeping
- claim forms
- adverse reaction forms
- yellow fever certificates.

Step 5: Travel healthcare

This identifies the systematic process of giving travel health advice in a consultation and should include:

- risk assessment
- immunisation
- health education
- returning traveller
- referral criteria.

Step 6: Monitoring and review

Details need to be included of the arrangements for evaluating and updating the clinical effectiveness and use of the protocol in practice from the point of view of both staff and travellers. Areas to consider including are:

- patient evaluation questionnaire
- audit
- communication channels for updating.

Step 7: Signing and dating

The protocol should be signed by all the healthcare professionals involved in providing the travel health service, in order to ensure that they understand and agree with the content. The protocol must be dated to make it a valid document.

Conclusion

The growth of Primary Care Groups whose main focus is towards the provision of services sensitive to the health needs of the local population, serves as an ideal opportunity for highlighting the need for a more rational approach to be taken to travel health through policy development and implementation. This would incorporate clinical governance in which Primary Care Groups are taking an active lead. An essential feature for this process of implementation would be ensuring all travel health service providers in primary care are working to comprehensive and quality driven travel health protocols. Besides supplying a framework for professional practice and service provision, they also provide an ideal format for risk management, by aiding the identification and reduction of professional, clinical and legal risks in general practice. The ultimate success of a protocol must lie in its ability to evolve continually with developments in health policy, professional practice, recommendations for the prescribing, supply and administration of medicines and to respond to changes in travel health.

Appendix

Information sources

Yellow fever centres

Application forms to become a Yellow Fever Vaccination Centre may be obtained by contacting the following:

England

Mrs Sue Doran
Department of Health
Room 601A
Skipton House
80 London Road
London
SE1 6LW
Telephone: 0171 972 5047

Scotland

Miss Carol Robertson
Scottish Office Department of Health
Public Health Policy Unit
Room 401
St Andrew's House
Edinburgh
EH1 3DI
Telephone: 0131 244 2278

Wales

Mr Adrian Preece
Public Health Division 3
Welsh Office
Cathays Park
Cardiff
CF1 3NQ
Telephone: 01222 82559

Northern Ireland

Mr Michael Kelly
Health Protection Branch
Department of Health and Social Services
Annexe 4
Castle Buildings
Stormont
Belfast
BT4 3RA
Telephone: 01232 520500

Yellow Fever Vaccination Certificates may be obtained by contacting:

Department of Health Publications Unit
PO Box 410
Wetherby
Yorkshire
LS23 7LN

Vaccine refrigerators

For advice on suppliers of suitable models contact:

Communicable Disease Branch
Department of Health
Area 708
Wellington House
133–135 Waterloo Road
London
SE1 8UG
Telephone: 0171 972 4472

Pharmaceutical Division
Scottish Office
Department of Health
St Andrew's House
Edinburgh
EH1 3DE

Computer databases

Travax online computer database

Information from the:
Scottish Centre for Infection and Environmental Health
Telephone: 0141 300 1100

Traveller computer database on disk

Information from:
Microdata I.T. Ltd
Telephone: 0114 285 4443

Useful internet sites

Eurosurveillance outbreak information

http://www.euroserv.org/main.htm

Foreign and Commonwealth Office

http://www.fco.gov.uk
Information on safety of travel abroad

International Society for Mountain Medicine

http://www.ismm.unige.ch
Society devoted to problems of high altitude medicine and physiology. Publishes a newsletter

International Society of Travel Medicine

http://www.istm.org
Includes the *Journal of Travel Medicine* (see *page 158*) and *Directory of Travel Clinics*

Liverpool School of Tropical Medicine

http://www.liv.ac.uk/lstm/lstm.html

London School of Hygiene and Tropical Medicine

http://www.lshtm.ac.uk/home.html

Travax online

http://www.axl.co.uk/scieh
The SCIEH database, now available on the Internet and NHS Intranet

Travel Health Online

http://www.tripprep.com
US database with much useful information, especially for US citizens

Travel Medicine News-share

http://www.istm.org/news_share.html
Edited in the UK, also accessible from ISTM website

US Centers for Disease Control

http://www.cdc.gov/travel/travel.html
Standard US travel information and advice

WHO disease outbreak information

http://www.who.ch/outbreak/outbreak_home.html

Other sources of help and information

Malaria

London School of Hygiene and Tropical Medicine
Public information line: 0891 600350 (24-hour access)
Healthcare professionals: 0171 636 3924 (09.00 – 16.30)

Travel health and safety information for healthcare professionals and patients

Academic Unit of Travel Medicine and Vaccines, Royal Free Hospital
Public enquiry line: 0891 633 433
Vaccination enquiries: 0171 433 1331
Healthcare professionals: 0171 794 0500

British Travel Health Association
4 Bedford Square
London WC1B 3RA
Telephone: 0171 255 1100
Membership is open to all healthcare professionals and others
with an interest in travel health

Department of Infection and Tropical Medicine, Birmingham Heartlands Hospital
Healthcare professionals: 0121 766 6611

Department of Infectious Diseases and Tropical Medicine, North Manchester General Hospital
Healthcare professionals: 0161 720 2677

Foreign and Commonwealth Office (advice on safety of travel abroad)
Public enquiry line: 0171 228 4503

Hospital for Tropical Diseases Travel Clinic
Public enquiry line: 0839 337733
Healthcare professionals: 0171 388 8989

Liverpool School of Tropical Medicine
Public enquiry line: 0891 172111
Healthcare professionals: 0151 708 9393

MASTA (Medical Advice Service for Travellers Abroad)
Public enquiry line: 0891 224 100
Healthcare professionals: 0171 631 4408

Public Health Laboratory Service, Colindale
Healthcare professionals: 0181 200 6868

Scottish Centre for Infection and Environmental Health
Healthcare professionals: 0141 300 1100

Advice for specific types of travel and travellers

Aid workers and expatriates

Corona Society
c/o Commonwealth Institute
Kensington High Street
London
W8 6NQ
Telephone: 0171 610 4407

Interhealth
Partnership House
Waterloo Road
London
SE1 8US
Telephone: 0171 902 9000

Air travel

For airport help for those with disabilities travelling from Heathrow
with British Airways:

British Airways Reservations, Heathrow
Telephone: 0181 749 8181

Air Transport Users Council
103 Kingsway
London
WC2B 6QX
Telephone: 0171 242 3882

For advice on disability and travel, and for crisis counselling for
travellers, including fear of flying:

Heathrow Airport Travelcare line
Telephone: 0181 745 7495

For airport help for those with disabilities travelling from Gatwick with BA:

> *British Airways Customer Care*, Gatwick
> Telephone: 01293 666224

For persons with disability and mobility problems using the North Terminal:

> *Airport Services*, Gatwick (North Terminal)
> Telephone: 01293 507147

For persons with disability and mobility problems using some airlines at South Terminal:

> *Airport Services*, Gatwick (South Terminal)
> Telephone: 01293 502337

For persons with disability and mobility problems using some airlines at South Terminal

> *Serviceair*, Gatwick (South Terminal)
> Telephone: 01293 505589

> *Aviation Health Institute*, Oxford
> Telephone: 01865 739 681

Asthmatic travellers

> *National Asthma Campaign*
> Providence House
> Providence Place
> London
> N1 0NT
> Telephone: 0171 226 2260
> Helpline: 0345 010203

Child travellers

Council for Disabled Children
8 Wakley Street
London
EC1V 7QE
Telephone: 0171 843 6000

*National Association for Maternal and Child Welfare
(NAMCW)*
40–42 Osnaburgh Street
London
NW1 3ND
Telephone: 0171 383 4117

Diabetic travellers

British Diabetic Association
10 Queen Anne Street
London
W1M 0BD
Telephone: 0171 323 1531

Disabled travellers

Disabled Living Foundation
Telephone: 0171 289 6111

Royal Association for Disability and Rehabilitation (RADAR)
Unit 12
City Forum
250 City Road
London
EC1V 8AF
Telephone: 0171 250 3222

Epileptic travellers

British Epilepsy Association
40 Hanover Square
Leeds
LS3 1BE
Telephone: 0113 242 8804
Helpline: 0800 309030

Expeditions

All types

Expedition Advisory Centre
Royal Geographical Society
1 Kensington Gore
London
SW7 2AR
Telephone: 0171 591 3030

Climbing

British Mountaineering Council Information Service
177–179 Burton Road
Manchester
M20 2BB
Telephone: 0161 445 4747

Female travellers

Corona Society
c/o Commonwealth Institute
Kensington High Street
London
W8 6NQ
Telephone: 0171 610 4407
Advice on living and working abroad for both male and female
travellers

Pregnant travellers

Royal College of Obstetricians and Gynaecologists
Telephone: 0171 772 6224
Leaflet on travelling in pregnancy

Travel insurance

Diabetic travellers

Information from British Diabetic Association (see *page 153*)

Expeditions

Information from *Expedition Advisory Centre* and/or *British Mountaineering Council* (see *page 154*)

Gay and/or HIV positive travellers

Positive Discounts
PO Box 347
Twickenham
TW1 2SN
Telephone: 0181 891 2561

Other pre-existing health problems

Positive Discounts (see above)
(Helpline in preparation for 'Freedom to travel' policy)

Personal and annual travel insurance

WEXAS International
45–49 Brompton Road
London
SW3 1DE
Telephone: 0171 589 3315

Travel insurance and special cases

Campbell Irvine Ltd
48 Earls Court Road
London
W8 6EJ
Telephone: 0171 937 6981

Books for the travel clinic library

A useful overview of travel health:

Walker (1997) *ABC of Healthy Travel.* 5th edition, Williams, Raeside and Calvert, BMJ Publishing Group, London

A comprehensive guide to health problems for travellers and their doctors:

Darwood R (1992) *Travellers' Health: How to stay healthy abroad.* 3rd edition, Oxford University Press, Oxford

A comprehensive introduction to tropical diseases:

Bell DR (1995) *Lecture Notes on Tropical Medicine.* 4th edition, Blackwell Science, Oxford

The essential UK immunisation:

DoH (1996a) *Immunisation against Infectious Diseases.* (the 'Green Book') HMSO, London

UK guide to health risks and vaccination for travellers:

Health Information for Overseas Travel. (1995) (the 'Yellow Book') HMSO, London

A slim country-by-country guide to risks, from the WHO:

International Travel and Health. (1997) World Health Organization, Geneva

A useful guide to risks for travellers with special health needs:

McIntosh IB (1993) *Health, Hazard and the Higher Risk Traveller.* Quay Books, Mark Allen Publishing, Salisbury

A comprehensive account of the problems of elderly travellers:

McIntosh IB (1992) *Travel Health in the Elderly.* Quay Books, Mark Allen Publishing, Salisbury

A definitive and detailed text from world experts:

Ward, Milledge, West (1995) *High Altitude Medicine and Physiology.* 2nd edition, Chapman and Hall Medical, London

A more manageable short introduction to high altitude problems:

Pollard, Murdoch (1997) *The High Altitude Medicine Handbook.* Radcliffe Medical Press, Oxford

A detailed 'bible' of tropical diseases:

Cook GC, ed. (1996) *Manson's Tropical Diseases.* Saunders, London

A guide to child and travel immunisation with some advice on travel health:

Kassianos G (1998) *Immunisation: Precautions and Contra-indications.* Blackwell Science, Oxford

Books for the traveller

A comprehensive guide to health problems for travellers and their doctors:

Dawood R (1992) *Travellers' Health: How to stay healthy abroad.* 3rd edition, Oxford University Press, Oxford

Guide for travellers, backpackers, volunteers and overseas workers:

(Includes a useful chapter on travel stress)
Lankester T (1995) *Good Health, Good Travel.* Hodder and Stoughton, London

Very practical advice from a doctor who has lived abroad:

Wilson Howarth J (1995) *Bugs, Bites and Bowels.* Cadogan, London

Simple advice on tropical illnesses, originally for health workers in developing countries:

Werner D (1985) *Where there is no Doctor.* Macmillan, London

Full of amusing and practical travel tips from an experienced traveller:
Hatt J (1993) *The Tropical Traveller*. Penguin, London

Information on just about every aspect of every kind of travel:
Haines M, ed. (1997) *The Traveller's Handbook*. 7th edition
WEXAS, London

A new American book from the Wilderness Medical Society:
Backer, Bowman, Paton, Steele *et al* (1998) *Wilderness First Aid
— Emergency Care for Remote Locations*. Jones and Bartlett
International, London

*A pocket-sized, comprehensive and well-established practical guide by a
former Everest doctor:*
Steele P (1988) *Medical Handbook for Mountaineers*. Constable,
London

*A practical, comprehensive and entertaining guide for parents by an
experienced parent and family traveller:*
Wilson Howarth J (1998) *Your Child's Health Abroad*. Bradt,
Chalfont St Peter, England

Travel medicine journals

Official journals of the International Society of Travel Medicine:

    Journal of Travel Medicine
    Decker Periodicals
    Hughson Street South
    PO Box 620
    Hamilton
    Ontario
    Canada
    L8N 3K7
    Telephone: (905) 522 7017

Travel Medicine International
Mark Allen Publishing Ltd
Croxted Mews
286a–288 Croxted Road
London
SE24 9BY
Telephone: 0181 671 7521

Suppliers of vaccines and travel-related products

Vaccine manufacturers and suppliers:

Medeva
Evans House
Regent Park
Kingston Road
Leatherhead
Surrey
KT22 7PQ
Telephone: 0345 451 500

Vaccine manufacturers and suppliers, including vaccine for Japanese B encephalitis:

Pasteur Merieux
Clivemont House
Clivemont Road
Maidenhead
Berkshire
SL6 7BU
Telephone: 03211 822 2463

Vaccine manufacturers and suppliers:

> *Smith Kline Beecham*
> Mundells
> Welwyn Garden City
> Hertfordshire
> AL7 1EY
> Telephone customer services: 01707 325 111
> Orders: 0800 716 280

Vaccine suppliers:

> *MASTA*
> Moorfield Road
> Yeadon
> Leeds
> LS19 7BN
> Telephone: 0113 239 1700

Suppliers of tick-borne encephalitis vaccine:

> *Baxter healthcare*
> Telephone: 01732 458101
> Orders: 01635 206046

A variety of travel-related goods:

> *Nomad Travel Pharmacy and Vaccination Centre*
> 3–4 Wellington Terrace
> Turnpike Lane
> London
> N8 0PX
> Telephone: 0181889 7014

Bed nets, insect repellents and other travel-related goods:

> *MASTA*
> Keppel Street
> London
> WC1 7HT
> Telephone public enquiry line: 0891 224 100
> Healthcare professionals: 0171 631 408

Ceramic water filters:

> *Katadyn*
> Telephone: 0300 30285

Bed nets, water purification devices and other travel related goods:

> *Cotswold*
> Broadway Lane
> South Cerney
> Gloucestershire
> GL7 5UQ (and branches elsewhere)
> Telephone: 01285 860612

Water purification devices:

> *Lifesystems Ltd*
> 4 Mercury House
> Calleva Park
> Aldermaston
> Berkshire
> RG7 4QW
> Telephone: 0118 981 1435

First aid and medical kits:

> *Philip Harris Medical Ltd*
> Hazlewell Lane
> Stirchley
> Birmingham
> B30 2PS
> Telephone: 0121 433 3030

Suppliers of screened blood for members to many but not all countries:

The Blood Care Foundation
PO Box 7
Sevenoaks
Kent
TN13 2SZ

Education in travel health

Diploma and MSc in Travel Medicine

University of Glasgow, one or two year distance learning course leading to Diploma or MSc. Information from:

Mrs Maria Williamson
Department of Public Health
1 Lilybank Gardens
Glasgow
G12 8RZ
Telephone: 0141 330 5617

Diploma in Travel Medicine

Royal Free Hospital. One year day-release course with PGEA and RCN accreditation. Information from:

Course Administrator
Academic Unit of Travel Medicine and Vaccines
Royal Free Hospital
Rowland Hill Street
London
NW3 2PF
Telephone: 0171 830 2999

Distance learning course

Magister Nurse Open Learning Programme. Information from:

> Freepost BS9133
> Frome
> Somerset
> BA11 1YA

Travel Health Promotion course for nurses

Day release course, ENB accredited. Information from:

> Jayne Archer
> Staffordshire University School of Health
> Blackheath Lane
> Stafford

Travel medicine course for practice nurses and GPs

University College of St Martin, Lancaster. Six months distance learning with thirty Level 2 credits or PGEA. Course material written by the author of this book. Information from:

> Linda Sharpe
> Short Courses Co-ordinator
> St Martin's College
> Lancaster
> LA1 3JD
> Telephone: 01524 384384

Further reading on policies and protocols

Howell K (1996)Accountability in travel health. *Practice Nursing* (8): 35–7

Montgomery J (1997) *Healthcare Law.* Oxford University Press, Oxford

References

Bolam v Friern Hospital Management Committee, 1957

Bradley DJ, Warhurst DC (1997) Guidelines for the prevention of malaria in travellers from the United Kingdom. *Communicable Disease Report.* Review 10: 137–52

Curtis C (1999) Personal protection against insect pests. In Dawood R (1999) *Travellers' Health.* Oxford University Press, Oxford

Department of Health (1991) *The Patient's Charter.* HMSO, London

Department of Health (1995) *Health Information for Overseas Travel.* (The 'Yellow Book') HMSO, London

Department of Health (1996a) *Immunisation against Infectious Disease.* (the 'Green Book') HMSO, London

Department of Health (1996b) *Primary Care: Delivering the future.* HMSO, London

Department of Health (1997) *The New NHS: Modern, Dependable.* HMSO, London

Department of Health (1998a) *A First-Class Service: Quality in the NHS.* HMSO, London

Department of Health (1998b) *Our Healthier Nation.* HMSO, London

Department of Health (1998c) *The review of prescribing, supply and administration of medicines: a report on the supply and administration of medicines under group protocols.* HMSO, London

Department of Health (1999) *Crown Report: review of prescribing, supply and administration of medicines: Final Report.* HMSO, London

European Union (1993) *The European Union Directive on Package Travel, Package Holidays, and Package Tours.* EU

Farthing MJG (1994) Travellers' diarrhoea. *Gut* **35**: 1–4

General Medical Council (1998) *Good medical practice.* General Medical Council, London

Mann JM, Chin J (1988) AIDS — a global perspective. *New England J Med* **319**: 302–3

Mehta DK ed, (1998) *British National Formulary.* British Medical Association, London and Royal Pharmaceutical Society of Great Britain, London

MORI (1996) *Health Research Survey.* MORI

NHS Executive (1996) *Promoting Clinical Effectiveness. A framework for action in and through the NHS.* NHSE, Leeds

Office of National Statistics (1995) *Travel Trends.* Office of National Statistics

RSL (1995) *Omnibus Survey.* RSL

Sane T, Koivisto VA, Nikkanen P, *et al* (1990) Adjustment of insulin doses of diabetic patients during long-distance flights. *BMJ* **301**(6749): 421–1

Steffen R, Fuchs E, Schildknecht J *et al* (1993) Mefloquine compared with other malaria chemoprophylactic regimens in tourists visiting East Africa. *Lancet* **341**: 1299–303

Steffen R, Lobel HO (1996) Travel Medicine. in: Cook GC, ed. *Manson's Tropical Diseases.* 20th edn, WB Saunders, London

Tingle J (1995) Clinical Protocols and the Law. *Nursing Times* **91** (29)

Townend M (1998) Sources and appropriateness of health advice for trekkers. *J Travel Med* **5** (2): 73–9

UKCC (1993) *Standards for the Spply and Administration of Medicines.* UKCC, London

Watkins P (1992) in Dawood R, ed. *Travellers' Health.* 3rd edn, Oxford University Press, Oxford

White M (1994) Personal Communication.

Wilsher v Essex AHA, 1988

World Health Organization (1996) *TB/HIV — a clinical manual.* WHO, Geneva

World Health Organization (1997) *World Health Report.* WHO, Geneva

World Health Organization (1999) *International travel and health: vaccination requirements and health advice.* WHO, Geneva

Index

A

A First-Class Service (DoH, 1998)
136, 165
abscess 106, 107
accidents 47–48, 95
acclimatisation
   to altitude 24–25
   to atmospheric pressure 29
   to heat 21
accommodation 7, 9, 11, 13, 31,
   34, 71, 96, 101–2
accountability 127–131, 134–135,
   141, 163
acetazolamide (Diamox) 25
active immunisation 62, 65
acute fever 106
acute mountain sickness 25, 38
adolescents 51
adrenaline 114
Africa 11, 13–14, 16–17, 19, 71,
   95, 97
African trypanosomiasis (sleeping
   sickness) 9, 18, 98, 108
aid workers 11, 50, 102, 151
AIDS (Acquired Immune
   Deficiency Syndrome) 11, 20, 54,
   74
air conditioning 101, 106
air quality 31
air travel 7, 28, 31, 36, 54, 100, 151
aircraft
   and malaria 6, 20
   and mobility 30–31, 40
   humidity 39
   pressurisation 28–30
airport malaria 20
airway 114

alcohol 3, 23, 30, 33, 39, 47–51,
   56, 101, 125
alternative regimen 83–89
altitude 13, 27, 48, 99
   acclimatisation to 24–25
   oxygen 24
   oxygen uptake 25
   problems 24
   sleeping 25
   threshold 24
American trypanosomiasis 9, 18,
   98, 108
amoeba 3, 5
amoebiasis 59, 109
amoebic liver abscess 107
anaemia 6, 8, 79
analgesics 27, 120
anaphylaxis; anaphylactic
   reaction/shock, 74, 114, 129, 134
Andes, Peru 24
angina 38
antibacterial drugs 4–5, 120
antibodies 61–63
antidiarrhoeal 4, 120
antigens 61, 62
antihistamines 33, 36, 114
anti-malarial
   doses for children 50, 81
   drugs 13, 43, 45, 49, 52, 59, 79,
      80, 89, 90, 120, 124
   precautions 35, 36, 59
   prophylaxis 8
   treatment 50
anti-mosquito precautions
   insect repellents 8, 9, 36, 66,
      91, 120, 161
   nets 8, 36, 66, 91–92, 101, 120,
      161

anti-mosquito precautions *(cont.)*
    in pregnancy 45, 50, 52, 80, 90,
        99, 155,
appointments system 113, 114,
    127, 141, 142
arborvirus 7
armies 54
Asia 7, 8, 13, 14, 15, 16, 17, 18,
    46, 53, 54, 56, 57, 66, 68, 69,
    87–89, 98, 99
asthma
    and high altitude 28
    and flying 31
    inhalers, problems with 43
    self-management 43
    steroid tablets 43
asthmatic travellers 28, 43, 152
atmospheric pressure
    and oxygenation 29
    and neonates 31
    and respiratory problems 28
    changes in 30
    falling 24, 28, 29
    on Everest 24, 28
audit 113, 123, 137, 138, 142

B

B cell lymphocytes 61
B cells 61
babies
    and gonorrhoea 58
    and herpes 57
    and pre-travel precautions 35
    and vaccines 98
baby foods 37
backpackers 50, 157
    accommodation 34
    and malaria 85
    and meningococcal disease 11
    and rabies 69
    sexually transmitted diseases
        34
backpacking 34
bacterial infection 107
barefoot 5, 37

bathing 102, 111
BCG vaccination 12, 63, 68, 71,
    74, 75
bicycles 47
Birmingham Heartlands Hospital
    150
bisexual men 54
bites 157
    bugs 9, 19
    fleas 9
    flies 8–9, 18, 36, 111
    insects 6, 13, 66, 110
    mammals 10, 17, 20, 69, 95
    mosquitoes 6–8, 13, 18, 36, 59,
        66, 77, 83, 86, 88, 90, 91, 92,
        101
    sea creatures 47
    ticks 9–10, 66, 106, 111
blindness 9, 45
blood
    clotting 27
    cultures 106
    diabetes 41–42
    donated 54
    dyscrasias 74
    film for malaria 79, 80, 105,
        109, 110
    frostbite 23
    high altitude 24–29
    HIV 54–56
    hookworm 6
    infected 6, 16, 19, 54, 68
    in stools 5, 108, 109
    malaria 77–80, 89, 105, 109,
        110
    passive immunisation 62, 63,
        65, 70
    pressure 21
    products 55, 68, 162
    strongyloides 6
    transfusions 54, 55
Blood Care Foundation 55, 162
body piercing 68, 110
Bolam Test 133
bone marrow transplantation 74

books
    for the traveller 157
    for the travel clinic library
        156–157
booster doses 62
bottle-fed baby 37
break-bone fever 6
breast-fed baby 37
breathlessness 26, 38
British Airways 151, 152
British Diabetic Association 40,
    46, 153, 155
British Epilepsy Association 154
British Mountaineering Council
    154
British National Formulary 35, 45,
    112, 114, 165
British Travel Health Association
    149
bronchitis 28
bronchodilators 40, 43, 114
brucellosis 108
bubonic plague 19
buffet food 4
bugs 9, 19, 157
bulk claim for vaccines 116
business travellers 41, 49, 54, 93,
    99

C

cabin air 30
Campylobacter 3, 109
Candida 59
carbonic acid 25
carcinoma of the cervix 57
casual sex 33, 34, 44, 47, 50, 53,
    56, 101, 102, 110, 112
cellulitis 106
Central America 13, 14, 15, 17, 98
cephalosporin 58
cerebral oedema 26–27, 38
Chaga's disease 18
chancroid 58
chemotherapy 74
Cheyne-Stokes 25

children 2, 6, 8, 11, 19, 22, 30, 31,
    35–7, 50, 51, 52, 53, 64, 68, 71,
    73, 74, 75, 80, 81, 82, 98, 130,
    153
    altitude sickness 37
    Eustachian tubes 36
    oral rehydration 37
China 14, 18, 88
Chlamydia 57
chloroquine 35,36, 43, 45, 81, 82,
    83, 84, 85, 86, 87, 88, 89, 90, 101,
    120
    epilepsy 43, 90
    + proguanil 85, 86– 87
    in pregnancy 45, 90, 99
cholera 2, 19, 63, 65, 109, 117, 119
    Peru 19
chronic diseases 100
    heart 9
    lung disease 38
cinnarizine 33, 36
ciprofloxacin 5, 49, 58
civil law 131
climate 13, 37, 96, 97
    cold 13, 23, 48
    hot 13, 17, 21, 34, 37, 39, 44,
        47, 48, 77, 100
    temperate 77
clinical effectiveness 123, 124,
    128, 136, 138, 140, 142
close personal contact vii, 10–12,
    16, 17, 34, 47, 53, 54, 56, 57, 65,
    67, 68, 102, 110, 111
Clostridium 108
cold 13
    conditions 48
    effects of 23
coma
    African trypanosoniasis 9
    heat hyperpyrexia 21–22
    high altitude cerebral oedema
        (HACE) 27
    Japanese encephalitis 8
    malaria 79
communications equipment 114

competence 32, 124, 129, 130,
131, 132, 133, 134
computer
access 113, 114
databases 13, 103, 113, 114,
147
condoms 53, 56
confidentiality 136
confusion 111
elderly 30
heat hyperpyrexia 21–22
hypothermia 23
malaria 79
consent 136
contra-indications to
anti-malarial drugs 90
flying 31
vaccination 43, 74, 134, 157
contract of employment 130
convulsions
due to mefloquine 90
in malaria 79
in reaction to vaccination 74
COPD 29
co-trimoxazole 5, 49
cough 11, 26, 28, 31, 106
counselling 50
prior to travelling 51
crash helmets 47
criminal law 131
Crown Review/Committee 135,
136
cruise ships 33, 101
cryptosporidium 3
culture shock 50–51
cyclizine 33

D

dairy products 4
ice-cream 4
databases 13, 103, 113, 114, 121,
147
deafness 45
deep vein thromboses 28
DEET 8, 91

dehydration 24, 27– 28, 30, 37, 39
due to high altitude 27
delegation of
immunisation 134
responsibilities 130
tasks 138, 139
travel health care 115, 133, 134
delirium 111
dengue 6, 15, 97, 106
risk to children 36
depression 51
due to mefloquine 90
dexamethasone 27
diabetic
British Diabetic Association
40, 42, 46, 153, 155
control 41–42, 153
insurance 40, 42, 153
travellers 41, 42, 153, 165
diarrhoea 4, 95, 108–109
chronic 5
in children 37
legionnaires' disease 106
malaria 79, 106, 108, 109
travellers' 3, 4, 95
treatment 4–5, 49, 120
typhoid 2
with blood in the stools 5, 108,
109
with blood in the stools and
fever 109
with fever 109
without fever 108
diarrhoeal diseases 108
diphenoxylate/atropine 4
diphtheria 12, 65, 102, 111
in former Soviet Union 12, 20,
97
diphtheria and tetanus vaccine
for adults (Td) 117
toxoid 64
vaccine/vaccination 12, 35, 63,
64, 67, 71, 72, 73, 117
direct liability 132
disabled travellers 45–46, 153

disabled travellers *(cont.)*
  children 153
  toilets 46
diseases of close personal contact
  10, 11, 12, 16, 17, 34, 47, 53, 54,
  56, 57, 65, 67, 68, 102, 110, 111
diuretics 26
diurnal rhythm 33
dogs 10, 17, 69
donated blood 54
doxycycline 36, 81, 83, 86, 89, 90,
  120
droplet infection 11, 12, 67, 100,
  102
drowning 33, 48, 102
drug prophylaxis in malaria 8, 13,
  36, 43, 45, 49, 52, 59, 79, 80,
  81–90, 93, 99, 101, 120, 124, 127,
  132
drugs
  antibacterial 4–5, 120
  anticonvulsants 43
  antidiarrhoeal 4
  anti-malarial 8, 13, 36, 43, 45,
    49, 52, 59, 79, 80, 81– 90, 93,
    99, 101, 120, 124, 127, 132
  anti-secretery 39
  diabetes 42
  hypothermia 23
  prescriptions 120
  storage 75, 114
  travel sickness 33, 36
duty of care 130, 132, 133

E

E coli 3, 109
ears 16, 22, 23, 29, 30, 32, 36, 100
eastern Europe 10, 18, 54, 66, 98,
  99
ebola 20
education in travel health 8, 123,
  124, 131, 137, 140, 142, 162
elderly travellers 24, 30, 31,
  38–40, 98, 100, 106, 157
electric vapourisers 92

electronic buzzers 92
elephantiasis 7
emerging and re-emerging diseases
  19
employees 49, 129, 130–131, 132
  137
employers 51, 129, 130–131, 132,
  134, 135, 136, 137, 140
eosinophil 6, 108, 112
  count 108, 112
epidemiology 124
epilepsy 43, 90
  chloroquine 90
  due to mefloquine 90
  Medic Alert 43
epileptic travellers 43, 90, 154
  anticonvulsant drugs 43
  diazepam 43
erythromycin 57, 58, 106
European Directives 126, 127, 165
Eustachian tubes 29, 30, 36
Everest 24
  atmospheric pressure 24, 28
exertion 24, 27, 28, 38
exhaustion
  heat 21
  hypothermia 23
  frostbite 23
expatriates 50, 51, 55, 56, 68, 80,
  101, 151

F

faecal-oral 14, 16
falciparum malaria 77, 78, 79, 81,
  90, 97, 99, 105, 110
Far East vii, 2, 97
febrile illness 74
  traveller with 105–106, 108
fees 116–121
female travellers 43–45, 98, 154
  casual sex 43, 102
  contraception 43, 44, 56
  pregnancy 31, 32, 44, 50–51,
    52
  STDs 57–58

female travellers *(cont.)*
  urinary tract infection 44
fever 105–8
filariasis 7, 18, 97, 107, 108, 111
first aid/sterile travel kits 43, 56,
  113, 114, 120, 161
fitness to fly 100
fleas 9, 34
flies 1, 4, 8–9, 18, 36, 91, 99, 111
fluke worm 2
flying
  advice 151
  asthma 31
  atmospheric pressure 28–30
  contra-indications 31–32
  elderly 38
  high altitude 24
  intraocular surgery 31
  jet lag 33, 41, 49
  mental illness 32
  neonates 32
  pregnancy 32
  previous medical history 29,
    30–32, 100, 112
  problems 28–33
  sickle-cell crisis 29
  tonsillectomy 31
food vii, 1, 4, 7
  and water hygiene vii, 1, 3, 14,
    34, 41, 65, 96, 100, 101, 102
  children 37
  diabetics 41–42
  elderly 39
  infants 37
  overindulgence 33, 49, 101
  poisoning 4, 47, 102
Foreign and Commonwealth Office
  148, 150
form GMS4 118–119, 121, 122
former Soviet Union 12, 20, 65,
  67, 97, 111
FP10 116, 117, 118, 120, 122
FP34D 117, 122
frostbite 23
frostnip 23

fruit 3, 37
frusemide 26
fungal infections 12

G

gastric acid 3, 39
gastrointestinal infections in
  children 98
Gatwick Airport 152
General Medical Council (GMC)
  130, 133, 165
general practitioner (GP) 12, 48,
  68, 105, 117, 121, 134, 163
genital warts 57
geographical patterns of disease 96,
  97–98
Giardia 3
giardiasis 59, 109
glucagon 42
GMS4 118–119, 121, 122
gonorrhoea 58
granuloma inguinale 58
'Green Book' 45, 114, 126, 156,
  165
guidelines
  for protocol 125, 128
  Scottish Health Board 121
  UK (Bradley) 83, 165
  UKCC 134
  WHO 125

H

H_2 antagonists 3, 39
  lansoprazole 39
  omeprazole 39
haemoglobin 25, 29
haemorrhagic
  fevers 6, 20, 111
  rash 106–107
Haiti 54
Haj pilgrimage 11, 68
hallucinations 111
  due to mefloquine 90
Hantavirus 19

headache 6, 7, 11, 25, 26, 27
health and safety 126, 130, 136
Health Authorities 116, 117, 119, 127
health education 8, 123, 124, 131, 137, 141, 142, 162
healthcare services 127
heart
    disease 9, 38, 95
    failure 38
heat 13, 21
    acclimatisation 21
    contraceptives 44
    effects of 21
    exhaustion 21
    hyperpyrexia 21–22
    prickly 21
    stroke 21
Heathrow Airport 151
hepatic failure
    in malaria 79
hepatitis A 2, 14, 16, 59, 63, 66, 70, 73, 95, 97, 101, 110, 119, 130
    distribution 15
    vaccination 65, 71, 73
    vaccine 35, 63, 65, 73, 98, 116
        in children 98
hepatitis B 15, 34, 47, 56, 63, 70, 72, 73, 97, 100, 101, 102, 110, 119
    distribution 16
    vacination 68
    vaccine 63, 68–69, 73, 116
hepatitis E 2, 110
herpes virus 57
heterosexual spread of HIV 54
high altitude 24–29, 37, 38, 44, 48, 77, 120, 148, 157
    cerebral oedema 26
    complications 26
    effects of 24
    pulmonary oedema (HAPE) 26
    travel 25
Himalayas, Nepal 24
hiring cars 47

HIV ix, 19, 20, 34, 44, 47, 53–56, 74, 97, 101, 102, 112, 155
    Africa 54
    AIDS 11, 19, 20, 54, 74
    and other STDs 55
    Europe 54
    non-sexual spread 55
    prostitutes 55, 56
    sexual transmission 19, 34, 56
    USA 54
holidays
    activity/adventure 48, 102
    backpacking 34
    package 34, 46, 48, 52, 126, 165
    trekking 24, 48, 68
homesickness 50
homosexual 19, 54, 56
hookworm 5, 37
Hospital for Tropical Diseases 150
host country viii–ix
hot climate 13, 17, 21, 34, 37, 39, 44, 47, 48, 77, 100
human papilloma virus 57
humidity 30, 39
hydrocortisone 114
hygiene vii, 1, 3, 14, 34, 37, 41, 44, 64, 65, 96, 100, 102, 148, 149
hyoscine 34
hypoglycaemia 41, 42
hypoglycaemic
    attacks 42
    drugs 42
hypothermia 23–24, 27, 33, 37, 48
hypoxia 25, 26, 27, 29, 31

I

ice 3
immobility 31, 34, 40, 44, 100
immunisation 13, 62–63, 64, 65, 70, 73, 114, 117, 126, 127, 129, 130, 134, 142, 156, 157, 165
immunity 2, 59, 61–62, 74, 80, 98
immunodeficiency 74

immunoglobulin 62, 63, 65, 70, 119
  IgG 62, 63
  IgM 62
  IgA 62
immunosuppressive treatment 74
impaired consciousness 111
impetigo 12
inactivated vaccines 62, 63, 65, 70, 74
India 12, 17, 18, 57, 66, 87, 95, 97, 99, 110
Indian subcontinent vii, 2, 10–11, 16, 66, 71, 106
indirect liability 132
infant feeding 37
inflammatory bowel disease 109
influenza 10, 79, 93
  vaccine 117
information leaflets 114
information sources 145–163
infrastructure 97
injecting drug users 8, 16, 19, 50, 52, 54, 55, 56, 68, 110
insects 34, 77, 101
  bites 6–10, 13, 18, 19, 36, 59, 66, 77, 83, 86, 88, 90, 91, 92, 101, 106, 110, 111
insect repellents 8, 9, 36, 66, 91, 120, 161
insecticide 8, 9, 92
insulin 41–42
  adjusting dosage 42, 165
  needles 42
  supplies 42
insurance 40, 46, 48, 155–156
International Certificate of Vaccination 7, 115
International Society for Mountain Medicine 148
International Society of Travel Medicine 148
internet sites 103, 148
intestinal parasites 112

intradermal injection 66, 69, 70, 75, 114
intramuscular injections 63, 64, 65, 66, 68, 69, 75, 114
intravenous drug users 8, 16, 19, 50, 52, 54, 55, 56, 68, 110
itinerary within the country 17, 25, 96, 99, 103, 107

J

Japan 10, 17, 66
Japanese B encephalitis 7, 17, 35, 63, 66–67, 98, 99, 100
  risk to children 36, 36
  vaccine 8, 63, 67, 72, 73, 118, 119, 159
jaundice 2, 79, 109–110
  in malaria 79
jet lag 33, 49
  in the diabetic 41

K

kala azar 18
knock-down insecticide 92

L

Lake Malawi 2
larva migrans 37, 47, 108, 110
Lassa 20, 106, 111
law 130–4, 163, 166
legal liability 131, 132, 136, 137
legality 135
Legionella 109
legionnaires' disease 106–107, 111
legislation 53, 125, 126, 127, 132
leishmaniasis 8, 18, 97, 107, 111
length of stay 13, 40, 49, 56, 96, 101
leprosy 12
leptospirosis 102, 107, 110
liability 131, 132, 136, 137
  vicarious 132
lice 9, 34, 59

litigation 137
live vaccines 44, 62, 63, 64, 66 70,
  74, 75
  in pregnancy 44, 74, 99
liver 8, 77, 78, 105, 107
  fluke 108
  function test 110
Liverpool School of Tropical
  Medicine 148, 150
London School of Hygiene and
  Tropical Medicine 148, 149, 150
long-distance travel 44, 55, 100,
  165
long-term travellers 17, 18, 50, 55,
  68, 69, 101
loperamide 4, 120
lower limb thrombosis 31, 38
Lyme disease 111
lymphangitis 111
lymphogranuloma venereum 57

M

malaria 6, 13, 18, 20, 36, 50, 59,
  77–93, 95, 99, 105, 106, 107, 109,
  110, 111, 127, 149
  avoidance of bites 6, 90, 91,
    101
  children 35, 50, 80, 81, 98
  clinical features 79
  diarrhoea 79, 106, 108, 109
  distribution 14, 99
  drug prophylaxis 8, 13, 36, 43,
    45, 49, 52, 59, 79, 80, 81–90,
    93, 99, 101, 120, 124, 127, 132
  expatriates 80
  hepatic failure 79
  hypnozoites 78
  immunity to 59, 80
  investigation of 79, 93, 106,
    107, 109, 110, 111
  jaundice 79
  non-drug prevention 35, 36,
    90–92, 93, 95, 101
  pregnancy 45, 50, 52, 80, 90,
    99, 155

malaria *(cont.)*
  prevention 81, 101, 121, 165
  self-treatment regimes 80,
    92–93
  standby treatment for adults 83
malaria parasites 80, 93, 105
  P falciparum 77, 78, 79, 81, 90,
    97, 99, 105, 110
  P malariae 77, 78
  P ovale 77, 78
  P vivax 77, 78, 105
malaria prophylaxis viii, 83, 101
  South Asia 87
  South-East Asia 88–89
  North Africa and the Middle
    East 83–84
  Oceania 86
  sub-Saharan Africa 85–86
Maloprim 36, 81, 82, 86
MASTA 150, 160, 161
Mecca 11, 68
Medic Alert 42, 43
medication 3, 32, 40, 41, 42, 43, 99
Medicines Act, 1968 131, 135
medico-legal 124, 129, 131–136
  implications 128
MEDIF form 40
mefloquine 35, 43, 49, 81, 82, 85,
  86, 87, 88, 89, 90, 101, 120, 124,
  132
  pregnancy 45, 90, 99
meningococcal 107
  disease 11, 17, 67, 68, 97, 98,
    100, 102
  in children 98
  infection 11, 67, 68, 98, 102
  vaccine 11, 35, 63, 68, 72, 73,
    116, 119
microscopy of stools 109, 112
middle ear 29, 30, 36
Middle East 8, 13, 14, 18, 54,
  83–84
migrants 54, 55
monitoring 135, 140, 142

mosquitoes 6–8, 9, 13, 14, 18, 20, 34, 36, 45, 59, 66, 67, 77, 78, 83, 86, 88, 90, 91, 92, 93, 100–101, 120, 161
   coils 92
   nets 8, 36, 66, 91–92, 101, 120, 161
motion sickness 33, 36
motor cycles 47
mountaineering 24, 48, 87, 99, 102, 148, 154, 155, 158
mucous membranes 28, 31
musculoskeletal problems 39
mussels 4, 47

N

National Asthma Campaign 152
nebuliser 114
needles 6, 42, 55, 56, 75, 114, 120
   sharing 19, 52, 54, 56, 68, 110
negligence 132
neonates 31, 32
Nepal 11, 17, 24, 38, 66, 68, 87, 97, 99, 110
neurological symptoms 9, 27, 67, 70, 111
   impaired consciousness 111
neuropsychiatric side effects of mefloquine 90
NHS Trusts 127
nifedipine 26
nightmares due to mefloquine 90
nitrates 40
non-A hepatitis 110
non-B hepatitis 110
non-drug prevention of malaria 35, 36, 90–92, 93, 95, 101
non-infective fever 108
non-reimbursible vaccines 118
non-sexual spread of HIV 55–56, 57
North Africa 14, 54, 83–84
North Manchester General Hospital 150

O

oedema 7, 26, 27, 30, 38, 39, 74, 79
onchocerciasis 8, 97
ophthalmia neonatorum 58
oral steroid therapy 74
oral typhoid vaccine 35, 63, 73
organ transplant 74
organising a travel clinic 121–122
osteoarthritis 39
overland travel 34, 100
   diarrhoea 34
   food 34
   personal hygiene 34
   vomiting 34
   water 34
oxygen 24, 25, 26, 29, 114
   in-flight 29
ozone layer 22

P

P falciparum malaria 77, 78, 79, 81, 90, 97, 99, 105, 110
Pacific region 15, 17
package holidays 35, 46, 48, 52, 126, 165
passive immunisation 62, 63, 65, 70
Patient's Charter 131
penicillin 58
permethrin 18, 92
   impregnated net 92
personal contact vii, 10–12, 16, 17, 34, 47, 53, 54, 56, 57, 65, 67, 68, 102, 110, 111
personal hygiene vii, 1, 34, 65
personality disorders 51
phenothiazine 23
photosensitive skin eruptions due to doxycycline 90
physical disabilities 40, 45–46, 151, 152, 153
plague 9
Plasmodium 77

plaster of Paris 31, 32
pneumococcal vaccine 117
pneumonia 28, 106, 111
policies 76, 115, 117, 121,
   123–143, 163
   and protocols 115, 123–143,
      163
poliomyelitis 2, 16, 44, 64, 65, 97
   in pregnancy 44, 74
   vaccination 35, 37, 64, 71, 72,
      73, 119
   vaccine 44, 65, 71, 73, 117
      inactivated 63, 64, 74
      live oral 63, 64, 71, 72, 74
polymorph count 106, 107, 108
poor vehicle maintenance 47
post-travel screening 112
potential sources of infection for
   children 37
practice nurse 12, 13, 48, 59, 71,
   105, 113, 115, 121, 130, 131,
   133, 134, 135, 139, 163
practice profile 128
pregnancy 31, 32, 44, 50–51, 52,
   99
   anti-malarial drugs 45, 50, 52,
      90, 99, 155
   chloroquine 45, 90, 99
   live vaccines 44–45, 74, 99
   malaria 45, 50, 52, 80, 90, 99,
      155
   venous thrombosis 44
Prescription Only Medicine (POM)
   120
Prescription Pricing Authority
   (PPA) 76, 116, 117, 118
previous medical history 8, 29,
   30–32, 51, 90, 96, 99, 110, 112
prickly heat 21
primary care groups 127, 131, 143
problems of backpacking 11, 50,
   69, 85
   food 34,
   sanitation 34

procedures 76, 115, 121, 122, 125,
   128–129
prochlorperazine 33, 36
proguanil 35–36, 45, 81, 82, 84,
   85, 86, 87, 89, 90, 101, 120
   in pregnancy 45
promethazine 33
Promoting Clinical Effectiveness
   (NHS Executive, 1996) 136, 165
prostitutes 53, 55, 56, 102
protocols 115, 121, 123–143, 163,
   166
   framework 124
psychiatric illness 32, 51, 90
psychosis due to mefloquine 90
psychotic illnesses 32, 51
public health 20, 96, 123, 130, 131,
   139
Public Health Laboratory Service
   117, 150
pulmonary
   alveoli 24
   artery pressure 26
   disease 11
   emboli 28
   infection 20
   in malaria 79
   oedema 26, 38

Q

quality assurance 128

R

rabies 10, 17, 69, 95, 96, 97, 112,
   dogs 10, 17, 69
   monkeys 17, 69
   vaccination 10, 69–70, 72, 75,
      100, 101, 119
      post-exposure 10, 69
      pre-exposure 10, 69
   vaccine 10, 63, 69, 70, 75, 100,
      117, 118
      post-exposure course 10,
         112

rabies *(cont.)*
    vampire bat 69
RADAR 153
radiation 74
railways 4, 45
raised temperature 21, 79, 105
rats 9
reciprocal healthcare arrangement
    46
recreational drugs 8, 19, 52, 54, 55,
    56, 68, 110
regular medication 40
rehydration 37, 39
    therapy 4
    sachets 120
reimbursement for vaccine fees
    116, 117, 118, 121
relapsing fever 107
relocating a family 51
remote areas 88, 100, 158
    travellers to 11, 68, 69, 100,
        101
renal function 39
repatriation due to illness 40, 46,
    48, 55, 95
respiratory symptoms 111
resuscitation equipment 114
returned traveller 105–112
returning home 12, 52, 54, 59, 80,
    105, 106, 131
rice paddies 8, 99, 100
rickettsial diseases 106
risk assessment 8, 95–104, 115,
    124, 142
risk management 137
river blindness 8
road traffic accidents 34, 47–48
Rocky Mountain spotted fever 9
rotavirus 3
Royal Free Hospital 149, 162
Royal Geographical Society 154

S

sailors 54, 55
salads 3, 65

Salmonella 2, 3, 107, 109
sandflies 8, 18, 111
    bites 111
sanitation 34, 65, 96, 97, 100
Saudi Arabia 17, 84
scabies 12, 59
Scandinavia 14, 18, 46, 66, 67, 98
schistosomiasis 2, 18, 97, 102, 108,
    109, 111, 112
Scotland 116, 121, 145
Scottish Centre for Infection and
    Environmental Health 103, 147,
    150
sea travel vii, 22, 33–34, 100–101
seafood 4, 47
self-treatment of malaria 80, 92–93
septicaemia 107
serological testing 106
    in HIV 112
serology 109
    hepatitis 110
    schistorumiasis 112
sewage 1, 14, 47, 64, 65
sex
    casual 33, 34, 44, 47, 50, 53,
        56, 101, 102, 110, 112
    industry 56
    safe practices 102
    tourism 8, 53, 102
    tourists 53, 102
    workers 53, 102
sexual
    offences 53
    transmission of HIV 19, 34, 56

sexually
    transmissible infections 53, 57,
        58, 59, 102
    transmitted diseases 16, 34, 44,
        47, 53–59, 68, 102, 155
sharing needles 19, 52, 54, 56, 68,
    110
shellfish 1, 47, 65
Shigella 3, 109
short business trips 5, 49, 85, 93

shower heads 106
sickle-cell crisis 29
sickle-cell disease 29
single component vaccines 62, 63, 70, 74
sinuses 29, 30
skiing 24, 48
skin 8, 18, 22, 77, 90
    ageing 22
    burning 22, 47, 100
    cancer 22, 47
    covering the 36, 66, 91
    infections 2, 5, 6, 9, 12, 47
    nodules 8, 58
    rash 110–111
    sutures 56, 120
    testing 68
    ulceration 12
smallpox 19
soil 5, 64, 110
sources of accidents 95
    alchohol 48
    badly-maintained cookers or heaters 48
    falling from hotel balconies 48
    road traffic 34, 47–48
    swimming and diving 48
South Africa 13, 14, 46, 86
South America vii, 2, 7, 8, 9, 13, 14, 15, 16, 17, 18, 19, 38, 54, 57, 66, 68, 69, 71, 95, 97, 98,
    high altitude 24, 38
South American trypanosomiasis (Chaga's disease) 9, 18, 98, 108
South and South-East Asia 7, 8, 13, 14, 15, 16, 17, 18, 46, 53, 54, 56, 57, 66, 68, 69, 87–89, 98, 99
Soviet Union 12, 20, 65, 67, 97, 111
spacer 43
Spanish conquistadores 19
spinal injuries 48
spread of HIV infections ix, 19, 44, 54–56, 97, 102

standards
    hygiene 3, 14, 34, 41, 44, 64
    of healthcare 123, 133, 134, 137, 138, 140
    of practice 115, 124, 125, 130, 133, 136, 137
    professional 130
    record-keeping 136
    safety in public life 97
    sterilisation/use of equipment 56
    vehicle maintenance 97
    for record keeping 136
statutory legislation 132
STDs and travel 16, 34, 44, 54–59, 68, 102, 155
sterile travel/first aid kits 43, 56, 113, 114, 120, 161
sterilisation 55, 56
stings 47
stock control 76, 117, 121
stool 4, 108, 109
    culture 5, 108, 109
    microscopy 109, 112
street stalls 4
stress 38, 39, 41, 43, 51, 90, 157
strongyloides 6, 37, 112
sub-Saharan Africa 11, 17, 68, 85–86, 97, 98, 105
sun 21, 33, 47, 48
    bathing 22
    burn 22, 47, 100
    children 37
    hat 22, 37
    screen 22, 37, 120
sunlight 21, 47
    effect of 21, 22
    exposure of skin 22, 47, 90
    UV radiation 22, 47
suppliers of vaccines 76, 115, 159–160
supply of vaccine 116, 117, 121, 135
surgery 31, 32

surgical procedures 16, 68
swimmer's itch 2, 111
swimmimg 2, 18, 91, 102, 111
    accidents 48
syphilis 58
syringes 42, 55, 56, 75, 114, 117,
    120

T

T cell lymphocytes 61
tanning 22
tattooing 16, 68, 110
teachers 11, 102
temperature
    body 31, 23, 79, 105
    climate 4, 77
    food 1, 4
    storage of medicines 42, 44, 75
tetanus 5, 64, 97
    toxoid 64
    vaccination 35, 64, 71, 72, 73,
        119
    vaccine 63, 64, 71, 73, 116, 117
tetracyclines 36, 57, 83, 90
Thailand vii, 53, 88, 89, 99
The New NHS: Modern,
    Dependable (DoH, 1997) 136,
    137, 165
thick film for malaria 80, 105
thin film for malaria 80, 105
thromboembolic disease 31, 98,
    100
thromboembolism 100
tick-borne encephalitis 10, 18, 66,
    67, 98, 99
        vaccination 67, 72, 73, 119
        vaccine 10, 63, 67, 73, 118, 160
ticks 9, 10
    bites 66, 106, 111
time of travel vii, 13, 71, 96, 100
topography 13
tour operators 40, 45, 46, 47
toxoids 62, 63, 64
trade routes 19
traffic 34, 43, 47–48

trauma 32, 33, 48, 57, 100, 102
Travax database 13, 103, 114,
    147, 148
travel
    clinic 13, 53, 56, 66, 68, 71,
        105, 113–115, 117, 118, 119,
        120, 121–122, 141, 148, 150,
        156–157
    consultations 102, 113, 114,
        128, 142
    insurance 40, 46, 48, 155–156
    journals 148, 158–159
    vaccinations 12, 14, 20, 35, 49,
        50, 52, 56, 61–76, 98, 99, 100,
        101, 115–119, 121, 122, 126,
        145, 146, 149, 156, 157, 160,
        166
        in Scottish practices 121
travel health service 113–122, 123,
    124, 126, 127, 128, 129, 130, 131,
    134, 137, 138, 139, 140, 141, 142
travel-related goods/products 120,
    159, 160, 161
Traveller database 13, 103, 114,
    147
traveller with diarrhoea 2, 3–5, 37,
    79, 95, 106, 108–109
travellers' diarrhoea 3–5, 49
    prevention 3–4
    treatment 4–5, 49
travel-related disease 1–34, 100
    causes of 96–97
trekkers 11, 69, 99
trekking 24, 48, 68
Trichomonas 59
tropical sprue 108
trypanosomiasis 9, 18, 98, 108
tsetse fly 9, 18
tuberculosis 11, 20, 67, 68, 102
tumbu fly 111
typhoid 2, 65, 66, 71, 95, 97, 106,
    111
    distribution 16–17, 97
    in children 35, 98
    vaccination 66, 71, 73, 119
    vaccine 35, 63, 65, 66, 71, 116,

typhoid *(cont.)*
   in children 35, 73, 98
      Vi antigen 63, 66, 71, 73, 98
      oral 35, 63, 73
typhus 9, 106

U

UK guidelines 83, 134, 165
UK immigrants
   returning home 12, 59, 80
UKCC 130, 133, 134, 135
ultraviolet (UV) 22, 47
upper respiratory 29
   infections 10, 11
   tract 28, 36, 100
   tract infection 29, 31
UV exposure 22
UV radiation 22, 47
UVA 22
   tanning/burning 22
UVB 22
UVC 22

V

vaccination vii, viii, 20, 43, 49, 50, 52, 61–76, 99, 121, 122, 126, 134, 149, 156, 157, 160, 166
   BCG 12, 63, 68, 71, 74, 75
   diphtheria 12, 35, 63, 64–65, 67, 71, 72, 73, 117, 119
   fees 116–119, 121
      payable by the patient 119
   hepatitis A 65, 71, 73
   hepatitis B 56, 68–69,72, 73, 101
   in pregnancy 74, 99
   Japanese encephalitis 8, 67, 72, 73
   meningococcal 11, 68, 72, 73
   of children 71, 73, 98
   polio 37, 64, 71, 72, 73, 119
   rabies 10, 69–70, 72, 75, 100, 101, 119

vaccination *(cont.)*
   schedules 70–71, 72
   techniques 75
   tetanus 35, 64, 71, 72, 73, 119
   tick-borne encephalitis 67, 72, 73, 119
   tuberculosis 68
   typhoid 66, 73, 119
   yellow fever 7, 14, 66–67, 70, 71, 72, 73, 115–116, 118, 119, 122, 145, 146
vaccine 6, 7, 43, 49, 59, 62, 66, 67–71, 72, 95, 101, 123, 125, 126, 127, 129, 134, 135, 149, 159–162
   BCG 12, 68
   cholera 63, 65, 117
   diphtheria 12, 63, 64, 71, 73, 117
   fees 116, 118, 119
   for children 35–36, 71, 73, 98
   hepatitis A 35, 63, 65, 73, 98, 116
   Hepatitis B 63, 68–69, 73, 116
   inactivated 62, 63, 65, 70, 74
   influenza 117
   in pregnancy 44–45, 74, 99
   Japanese B encephalitis 8, 63, 66, 67, 73, 118, 159
   live 44, 62, 63, 64, 66, 70, 74, 75, 99
   meningococcal 11, 35, 63, 68, 73, 116
   ordering of 76
   plague 9
   pneumococcal 117
   polio 44, 63, 64, 65, 71, 73, 74, 117
   problems 71, 74
   purchase of 76, 116, 117, 118
   rabies 10, 63, 69–70, 75, 100, 112, 117, 118
   refrigerators 75–76, 114, 115, 146, 147
   reimbursement 116, 117, 118, 121

vaccine *(cont.)*
  single component 62, 63, 70, 74
  stock control of 76
  storage of 75–76, 115
    temperature 75
  suppliers 76, 115, 159–160
  supply 116, 117, 121, 135
  tetanus 63, 64, 71, 73, 116, 117
  tick-borne encephalitis 10, 63, 66, 67, 72, 73, 118, 160
  tuberculosis 12, 68
  typhoid 35, 63, 65, 66, 73, 98, 116
  yellow fever 35, 36, 44–45, 63, 66–67, 71, 73, 74, 98, 115, 118, 119
Valsalva manoeuvre 30
venous thrombosis 31, 38, 44
vicarious liability 132
viral
  haemorrhagic fevers 106, 111
  infection 106, 108
  respiratory infections 111
visceral larva migrans 108
vivax malaria 77, 78, 105
voluntary aid work 11, 50, 102, 151

W

wall chart 103, 115
water 1–2, 3, 8, 9, 18, 21, 22, 23, 27, 77
  bottled 3, 4, 37
  hygiene vii, 1, 3, 14, 34, 37, 39, 41, 47, 64, 65, 96, 97, 100, 101, 102, 111
  purifying equipment 3, 120, 161
  sports 47, 48, 102, 110
water-borne infections 102
West Africa 18, 95, 101
wheelchairs 39, 45, 46
white cell count 106, 109, 110
white water rafting 102

working abroad 9, 10, 11, 17, 49–52, 65, 69, 101, 102, 117, 151, 154, 157
World Health Organization (WHO) 19, 65, 115, 149, 125, 156, 166

Y

'Yellow Book' 114, 126, 156, 165
yellow fever 7, 67,
  distribution 14, 15, 97
  in pregnancy 44, 74, 99
  vaccination 7, 14, 66–67, 70, 71, 72, 73, 115–116, 118, 119, 122, 145, 146
  Vaccination Centre 66, 115–116, 118, 122, 145
  vaccination certificate 7, 14, 119, 142, 146
  vaccine 35, 36, 44–46, 63, 66–67, 71, 73, 74, 98, 115, 118, 119
young children
  food and water hygiene 37

Z

zopiclone 33